Stephen is a living example of inner transformation and an inspiration to anyone who has struggled with depression. His book stands as testimony that, with commitment and perseverance, we can all find the joy and fulfilment we seek.

—Isha Judd, humanitarian and bestselling author of *Why Walk When You Can Fly?*

NO STONE UNTURNED

The Path to Freedom

Stephen Connor

BALBOA
PRESS
A DIVISION OF HAY HOUSE

Copyright © 2014 Stephen Connor.

All rights reserved. No part of this book may be used or reproduced by any means, graphic, electronic, or mechanical, including photocopying, recording, taping or by any information storage retrieval system without the written permission of the publisher except in the case of brief quotations embodied in critical articles and reviews.

Balboa Press books may be ordered through booksellers or by contacting:

Balboa Press
A Division of Hay House
1663 Liberty Drive
Bloomington, IN 47403
www.balboapress.com.au
1 (877) 407-4847

Because of the dynamic nature of the Internet, any web addresses or links contained in this book may have changed since publication and may no longer be valid. The views expressed in this work are solely those of the author and do not necessarily reflect the views of the publisher, and the publisher hereby disclaims any responsibility for them.

The author of this book does not dispense medical advice or prescribe the use of any technique as a form of treatment for physical, emotional, or medical problems without the advice of a physician, either directly or indirectly. The intent of the author is only to offer information of a general nature to help you in your quest for emotional and spiritual well-being. In the event you use any of the information in this book for yourself, which is your constitutional right, the author and the publisher assume no responsibility for your actions.

Any people depicted in stock imagery provided by Thinkstock are models, and such images are being used for illustrative purposes only. Certain stock imagery © Thinkstock.

Printed in the United States of America.

ISBN: 978-1-4525-2650-8 (sc)
ISBN: 978-1-4525-2651-5 (e)

Balboa Press rev. date: 11/17/2014

To Dianne, for your love and support

To my beautiful family, I love you all

*The greatest gift you can
give is the internal love
you are constantly nurturing.*

Contents

Preface ix
Acknowledgements xv

Part 1. A Guide for Emotional Healing and Mental Health

Introduction 3
Tools for Mental Maturity, Growth, and Well-Being ... 11
My Exercises 51
An Awakening 55
Spirituality 71

Part 2. A Spiritual Journey

Introduction 77
Chapter 1   Humble 79
Chapter 2   Value 83
Chapter 3   Wake Up Sleeper 93
Chapter 4   Life 103
Chapter 5   Harvest 111
Chapter 6   Rest 121
Chapter 7   Fire 129
Chapter 8   Just Be 135
Chapter 9   Choice 143
Chapter 10 Share 147
Chapter 11 The Afternoon 153
Chapter 12 Life Is a Game 159

Afterword 161
About the Author 165

Preface

There is a reason why you are holding this book in your hands. The reason could be one of many. You may be going through a turning point in your life or a crisis, or you may be searching for something different. Or maybe you are just curious with instincts that seem to be guiding you in some way.

There is a common trait that drives us all, and that is the strong urge to be "more" and evolve. By *more* I mean to be progressive and be the best we can. This instinct led me on a journey to the opening of my heart and to a clearer perspective. The journey would not have been possible if I had kept rejecting my heart's calling. The key to this opening has been the will to change and to take the necessary steps to end my suffering and finally follow my heart.

This book is about finding self-love and how appreciating yourself is the beginning to this discovery. You are richer than you think, and I hope you feel that now as you give gratitude for who you are and the life you have experienced. Self-love and appreciation are true riches; they are your true nature beneath wherever your mind and thoughts take you.

Thoughts are the genesis of life's dramas and dreams. They are the co-creators of the scenarios and mental movies we direct and produce in our minds. As the directors and producers of these movies, we have the power to change how they unfold. If we are aware of this power and how deeply our thoughts affect us, we can control what role we play in each scene.

There were many moments when my thoughts were obsessively soul destroying and self-sabotaging. They created a false reality in which I played only a minor role in the movie of my mind. This role was one of survival in which I would unconsciously camouflage my negative thoughts and emotions in an attempt to live a happy life. True reality is the major role I can now play in a film called *Thriving—Not Surviving*.

Thoughts can create an internal turmoil that is difficult to detect until some form of crisis occurs. My crisis came when my self-sabotaging thoughts eventually pushed me into the dark hole of depression. This led me on a search for something different, and thankfully, I started to find how love can change your life. Self-love and appreciation are the most precious gifts you can give to yourself, and my hope is that this book will help you open up these gifts.

This book is divided into two parts. The first is about my story and recovery from deep depression. This was both a frightening ordeal and a life-changing experience. As I recovered, I wrote down all the tools I had learned. The more I wrote, the better I felt. This inspired me to develop more, and that is how this book evolved.

The second part of the book is a combination of my poetry and my spiritual journey and where that path has taken me. My poetry comes from my own unique experiences and the insights that came on the way. On my journey I have discovered the important things in life. It is a journey that continually teaches me about the most valuable thing of all, and that is love. It is through my life experiences—past, present, and future—that love will grow. Poetry has given me an avenue to express this.

I have left the first part in the same basic format that I wrote back then with the same perspective I had at the time. For those who are in a depressed state, my hope is that you can relate to this perspective. If you adopt a positive attitude, depression can be the beginning of a new way of life and not just an experience you survive. There have been many others like me who have taken the sense of hopelessness that comes with depression and turned it into a life full of opportunities. For those who seek the fulfilment of living a full life, my hope is that this book inspires you to do just that.

When in depression, your emotions become raw, and even though they are mostly unpleasant, they are fully exposed, waiting to be expressed. These emotions have been suppressed for a long time, and they contribute to a feeling of low self-esteem and the suffering this brings.

When emotions are raw, they can be clearly seen, which presents an opportunity to finally face them. It does take courage and commitment, but the benefit is the end of suffering, and this is freedom. It is simply a matter of what life you choose to live.

Choices are mainly emotionally driven and have a real personal power attached to them. Coming out of a depressed emotional state is about making choices that are in your best interest. To realise this is empowering. When I was at my lowest point, I became frustrated and confused with people trying to make choices for me, so I started to make my own decisions and learned from the experience. The best decision I made was to live and do whatever it took to enjoy a full and happy life.

With a willingness to bring more love into your life, the awareness of your feelings will grow as well. This awareness manifests when you are committed to doing whatever it takes to change. One of the best changes that happened to me was letting go of the past and living in the present. The spiritual practice that I committed to has helped me in this goal. I found this practice when I was determined in my search to live the best life I could. It is called the Isha System, and I will talk more about it throughout the book.

It is common for people who have gone through a crisis or deep depression to embark on a search and discover more of life. It is a journey that does not end but just keeps evolving. The most important aspect of whatever path or practice you choose is the commitment to that part of you that you can fully rely on, and that is the belief and trust in yourself. This is difficult to do if you are in an anxious and confused state, but if you keep focusing your attention on that belief, it will grow. Whatever you focus your attention on will grow. This is just the natural progression of life.

Acknowledgements

My Teachers

There are always people you want to thank when you make it through a particularly hard time in your life. They give you support when you need it most, and it is important to take the opportunity of support when it is there. My opportunity came in the form of a wonderful man, my therapist, Tom. A lot of what I write about is based on my time with Tom and the insights I have gained since. I hope you all have an opportunity to have a man like him in your life.

There were times when I did doubt his approach to my time in deep emotional pain. Those around me questioned his type of therapy, as I seemed to fall further into depression. This made it even more difficult to keep at it, but thankfully, I did. It basically felt right. Thanks, Tom.

Thank you to all the health professionals that gave me warmth and attention when I needed it.

To Isha and her wonderful teachers, the love that you give is abundant and unconditional.

PART 1

A Guide for Emotional Healing and Mental Health

Introduction

When life takes an unexpected turn, we can sometimes be caught in the grip of deep emotional pain and suffering. This can put us in the downward spiral of depression and anxiety. For some, the confusion of not knowing what is happening and what to do about it can be overwhelming, and this can increase the anxiety. With my story and the tools that I developed, my aim is to give you the inspiration to see any painful situations as opportunities for learning and growth. I like to think of my story as a guide because support and guidance will help you find the internal strength you need to do whatever it takes to live a happy and healthy life.

Throughout this guide I have tried to keep to a minimum the words used in the diagnosis of what is called mental illness. Words have power, and when we are in a vulnerable state, it can be quite easy to attach a diagnosis to our identities. My fear and anxiety increased when I was diagnosed, and this gave me a feeling of isolation. I felt there was something seriously wrong with me, and it is important not to feel this way.

There is a need to break down the barriers and stigmas surrounding mental health. Mental illness generates fear. When people are diagnosed and labelled, they can slowly become the diagnosis, and this increases the fear. This was the case for me as my attitude changed overnight after I was told I had major depression. As my condition declined, the labelling and diagnoses increased with bipolar and possible personality disorder being added.

Psychological diagnosis can be a very grey area with no real delineation. Statistics show us that mental ill health is a growing major concern, and sadly more and more people are suffering under its effect. This is an indication that a more refined approach and understanding is needed. An extreme case of mental instability requires a logical and objective professional assessment, but in general, is diagnosis creating a false perception to an already confused mind? By adding the deeper component of spirituality to the process, our understanding will accelerate significantly. Spiritual psychology will help us advance to a clearer and purer perspective.

Recently, I saw a documentary about the development of psychology and the experiments that were carried out on both humans and animals in an attempt to try to understand and gain a cure for depression and mental illness. A psychologist said that the experiments, even though horrific at times, were worth it if a cure for mental illness was found. I think that a simple yet important point is being missed here. A cure need not be the main objective, as it implies that something is wrong or needs fixing. There is nothing wrong, even if there are times when you think you are going crazy. This is just a result of the intellect or the mind that has been in command for a long time and wants to keep this dominance firmly in place.

The word *illness* imprints fear in our minds, and this affects how we relate to others. Being diagnosed with a mental illness can increase our isolation. Our true mental state can then be suppressed with the real person hiding behind the fear. This creates a stigma and something to be avoided. If we are not real with ourselves and our own emotions, we leave the real person somewhere inside a fear-driven image. It might seem strange, but it is as if we develop into two people. We become separate from our childlike, true nature. To heal this separation is a true expression of ourselves and our lives.

Creating a society that works towards feeling all there is to feel and not labelling and diagnosing would put us on a path of unity and growth. The fact is at some time in our lives, we all experience some form of emotional pain; it is part of the human condition. It is the mindset we have created in the human condition of good or bad, better or worse, and right or wrong that inhibits unity and our growth. Being right means something or someone else is wrong, and we set up a court of law in our minds where judgements and analysis create confusion. Shakespeare wrote in *Hamlet*, "There is nothing either good or bad, thinking makes it so."

Our mental state and the accompanying emotions are our opportunities to a better understanding of ourselves, and with that we can use the emotions in our growth towards emotional maturity. With the passionate intention to feel all emotions, especially the painful ones that come with a depressive state, we can *create* a purpose and meaning from them. As humans we have been blessed with an abundance of emotions that are largely undervalued. If we break the fear surrounding mental health and give support, understanding, and compassion to those who are in deep emotional pain, we will *all* benefit.

There is wonderful support already in the mental-health industry, but it is mainly geared towards getting people *better*. Again, this implies there is something *wrong*. The reality is that emotions and the pain that sometimes comes with them are part of life. What is needed is to show those in *deep* emotional pain how to process their emotions and use them as an opportunity and a guide towards clearer decision-making and more insight. With more insight and understanding to what is happening right now, the present moment can be seen as just perfect in any circumstance.

When in deep emotional pain, the present moment seems anything but perfect, and this is where a change in focus is needed. The change can be terrifying at times because the mind tends to resist change. Letting go of the old ways and the voice in your head, the voice that has directed you all your life, is usually very scary indeed. The recognition for change is important, followed by a strong *will* to take the necessary steps to change.

From my experience, not enough is said about this stage of change. Mostly people just want to get back to their normal lives and escape from the pain as quickly as possible. The paradox is if the work is *not* done, escaping from painful emotions will always create more suffering. The emotions stay lodged and unprocessed, and an opportunity is gone. The work needed can be challenging, messy, and stressful but also, as I found after only a few months, very rewarding.

We all have been through many life situations or cycles of life—some are micro-cycles lasting short periods, and some are macro-cycles lasting for quite a bit longer. It is beneficial to realise that these cycles come and go, and if you are suffering deeply now, just be assured that this cycle will pass. What choices you make while in this cycle will determine what insight and how much emotional growth will be added to your life.

My life was quite a normal one, and I made all the usual choices. I grew up in a working-class area, had lots of friends, and pushed the usual boundaries of an energetic boy. I got married young and worked hard, and life seemed perfect until I suffered what is commonly called a breakdown in my late twenties. After recovering reasonably well I sustained a happy life bringing up two wonderful children and managing to stay married for over thirty years. I prefer to use the term *broken open* now instead of *breakdown*, as the term *breakdown* implies something is wrong; the reality is, there is nothing wrong. Being *broken open* is like a seed breaking open and flowering with an opportunity for future growth.

Keeping on top of my anxiety was always a constant battle, and this was mixed with minor bouts of depression. I had many different jobs and was always trying to better myself and just enjoy life. After about thirty years, my marriage finally ended, and I set about trying to create a new life. I did quite well, I thought, until I fell into a major depressive state. I became more and more anxious until I became hospitalised and was very close to suicide on a few occasions. I had different types of therapy and eventually went on medication for a short period. I could write more about my story, but I will leave that for later. The main thing to know is that there is an end to the pain that comes with depression and that peace is close by.

In this guide, I will give you my experiences and the tools that I developed to gain control of my life and mind. There are also exercises I used to help me gain emotional release and clarity in my decision-making. I give insight into how my time in crisis and deep emotional pain turned into an opportunity to change and start realising my true nature and potential. It has been a challenging and yet a wonderfully rewarding experience and a journey that has given me true meaning and purpose.

The tools I discuss will help you understand your pain and suffering, and that will set you on a path to gain peace and happiness. You definitely have the courage and the strength to achieve this. No matter how much you search, the thing that will start you on the road to recovery is the realisation that you have the inbuilt abilities to bring joy into your life. Be prepared to try everything available, and be gentle on yourself in the process. Be open to new ideas, commit to changing the way you think and do things, and leave *No Stone Unturned*.

When you are inspired by someone look deeply into a mirror, there is inspiration there as well.

Tools for Mental Maturity, Growth, and Well-Being

- emotional awareness
- daily ritual
- spirituality
- intuition
- choice
- judgements, assumptions, criticism, and comparisons
- truth
- theory
- blame and responsibility
- experience
- belief and faith
- acceptance
- gratitude
- expression
- planning
- problem-solving
- mood management

- negative-thought management
- mindfulness and focusing
- exercise and physical health
- yoga
- body awareness
- healthy eating
- group therapy program
- giving to others
- self-pity
- pride and dignity
- courage and strength
- happiness
- openness and friendliness
- simplicity
- relaxation
- positivity
- accepting and giving love freely
- creativity and imagination
- moral awareness
- assertiveness
- medicines
- acupuncture
- massage
- music
- aromas
- maintenance
- support
- laughter
- counselling
- love and compassion

All these tools were developed in my recovery from depression. There have been many influences in their development, and they are not part of any specific therapy or spiritual practice. I have tried to explain them in an honest and personal way and not be patronising. There are many wonderful therapies and spiritual practices available, and finding one that suits you can be time-consuming. I hope this guide helps and inspires you in your search to find your own unique process.

Never stop learning.

Emotional Awareness

Emotions are our doorway to a new way of thinking and a new way of life. They are not to be judged, just accepted as part of growth towards mental maturity. Being in touch with emotions and understanding them is challenging, but it is the first step to mental well-being. I use emotions now as a guide to the way that I express myself in relationships and the many situations that arise in everyday life.

Many emotions are triggered on a constant basis—anger, sadness, disappointment, guilt, fear, envy, jealousy, pity, love, joy, and compassion. These all have to be felt and understood. The more you are in tune with and recognise emotions, the more you will understand the triggers.

Once felt and recognised, emotions need to be therapeutically processed; otherwise the emotions that bring us pain will build up inside and manifest sometime in the future, usually causing some type of suffering. By *therapeutic* I mean emotions need to be felt for a short period in a *controlled* and *aware* manner. We like feeling the pleasurable emotions but are usually poor at feeling the hurtful ones.

Once emotions are processed, coming back to the present is essential. It is the focus and attention you give to the present moment that is important. To be content with the acceptance of each moment, whether pleasant or unpleasant, is difficult, but it is a goal well worth striving for.

I was surprised at how little I understood and recognised my emotions and how constantly my thoughts went from the past to the future with hardly any attention to the present. After a while I became more aware of my emotions and the situations, both past and present, that triggered them. With practice, I was then able to open up the doorway to the joy of just being in the moment.

We all have been hurt in some form or another from an early age, and up to around the age of five, we had our own unique abilities to process our hurt naturally. We may have thrown tantrums out of frustration, cried for no particular reason, or just hugged our mothers for warmth and love. As we became more aware of what society and our culture expected of us, those abilities slowly diminished. Our image and identity develop with emotions building up inside, creating our personalities.

To process emotions now, I talk them through, write about them, cry if I feel the need to, scream into a pillow, or just reflect on the emotion using some of the knowledge that I have absorbed in workshops I have attended and in the books I have read. It does take time for this knowledge to be absorbed, so it is important to give yourself that time and above all be gentle on yourself. The more I felt all my emotions and stopped resisting them, the clearer my thoughts became, and with this came clarity in my decision-making. Emotions are now my guiding force; they are a hidden treasure.

Daily Ritual

I have found it is important to have a daily practice or ritual in which I take time out for myself to do the emotional work. It is an opportunity to clear all the emotional baggage and not let it build up. Doing some form of meditation and affirmations after the clearing work helps in self-awareness. Simple affirmations are a good starting point in any daily ritual. These include the following: "I am worthy," "I believe in myself," "I choose to become more aware as I go through this cycle," "I choose peace, calm, and love," and "I choose to let the cares of the world fade away." In between saying these, sitting silently for a few minutes and watching your thoughts is beneficial. As you watch your thoughts, do not judge them, but just let them pass by. This will help in not judging and being hard on yourself. Judging and criticising ourselves and others is soul destroying and benefits no one.

If anxiety and lack of energy make it difficult to concentrate, there is usually a time in the day when we can sit and contemplate even if only for a few minutes. My ritual now can vary from about twenty minutes to an hour depending on how I feel. I sit down somewhere quiet and go inward. Whatever emotions arise I feel and express them. Quite often there is sadness under all the emotions, and I gladly let the tears flow. Having someone to share these moments with is important as you become more aware of your feelings. After this emotional release I then focus on being present by enjoying and appreciating life.

Strangely, there is not a lot known about why we cry, but I find that it breaks down the hard shell that I formed in early childhood. The shell was my mechanism for coping, and now as time goes by, the shell falls away slowly, and my heart opens up. As my heart opens up, so does my life. My creativity, intuition, and belief in myself keep expanding.

My daily ritual has changed over the years, and as a facilitator for the Isha System, I am glad to teach this process to anyone who is ready to truly follow his or her heart. I make many references throughout the book about the system, so you will get a general idea about it as you read, or you can visit the website (www.ishajudd.com).

Spirituality

This has become an important tool for me now. Five years ago, I did not really understand what spirituality meant. For me now, it means to bring the spirit part of mind, body, and soul more into my life. There are many ways to explain what spirituality means. A simple way is to say it brings more awareness and consciousness in one's life.

Being aware and spiritually conscious of your thoughts, expression, and actions is such a wonderful tool to have. It gets hard and challenging sometimes but is definitely worth it. Your life so far has probably been hard and challenging, but with more awareness, you will develop more direction and add purpose and meaning to that life.

The word *spirituality* can often be taken out of context and can get confused with religion, so I have given just a brief outline on it here and have written more on it at the end of this guide. There is a truth in all religions, and it is spirituality that exposes this truth.

Intuition

Intuition is such a wonderful part of us, but if there is a lack of belief and faith in oneself, this beautiful natural ability is never accessed. From time to time I would use my intuition, but I was not aware of its full potential. As I became more aware of it, I trusted in my decisions, and this gave me greater feeling of self-belief.

Going with these feelings and using your intuition is about following your heart. Try to use your intuition to help make clearer choices. Basically, if someone gives you advice and it feels right, go with that feeling. Your intuition and therefore choices can guide you on what advice you absorb and what actions you take.

Choice

Choice is powerful. Be careful with this tool, and try not to make too many important choices while in deep emotional pain. I made some disastrous choices when I was very confused, and that put me deeper into the hole of depression.

Emotions and choices go hand in hand; the more emotionally mature you become, the more confident you become with choices. Doing the simple things first and just thinking about your decisions calmly will stop the addition of more suffering in your life. When the pain eases and clarity comes, your choices will become very powerful indeed. Try to be patient.

Judgements, Assumptions, Criticism, and Comparisons

We tend to be overly judgemental and critical of every aspect of our lives, and being too hard on ourselves is quite common. When we add the paranoia of assumptions we can become very confused if we rely on the responses of others. If we then make comparisons the confusion magnifies.

Trying to assume what others are thinking is such a waste of time, and quite often, the person is not thinking what you have conjured up in your mind anyway. You are your own unique self, and comparing yourself or your situation to others and making assumptions will just create more suffering. The answer is just to be yourself.

The easiest way I found to begin to take control of judging was to look at the way I judged others and in turn become more aware of the way I judged myself. It is difficult to stop all our judgements completely, but becoming aware of certain ways we judge is a healthy way to raise our self-esteem, especially if combined with the next tool.

When I feel myself judging, I just think, *Oh, here I am judging again. How interesting.* If you do this, you tend to stop the vicious circle of being too hard on yourself and being critical of others. With less judging, your assumptions and comparison will lessen as well.

Truth

The truth of who we are and can be is always with us; it is the search and discovery of this truth that will manifest if we do the emotional work to expose that truth. The challenges and crises in our lives can be opportunities to find the truth. They are the catalysts for change—change in the way you think, express yourself, and take actions. Truth means to be true to yourself and your emotions and to others.

Theory

Theory and what you practise should go together to provide you with a clearer understanding of what is happening to you. The theory of basic psychology and how the brain and mind work is helpful in this understanding, and if you balance it with a daily ritual, the benefits will come. Be prepared to learn about basic psychological functioning.

Automatic behavioural patterns are formed from early childhood. We work out ways to understand and cope with the world around us, and these form our personalities. The neural pathways that link our brain and body are in a constant state of design and repair. They can become heavily clogged with emotional build-up. The clearer these pathways are, the more you will free your mind and gain confidence and understanding, especially over your fears.

Fears attach to us throughout our lives, and they are all linked. Learn as much as you can about mental health, and though it might not seem like it, it is worth the effort. You will pick up little things as you go and reap the rewards as you become more mentally mature. Mental health is such a grey area, so be confident in yourself to use what you learn, and form your own opinions in a practical and beneficial way. There are many books on mental health in your local library.

The more I learned about the theory of the mind and the brain, the more I wanted to absorb. I went back to college after I became clearer and obtained a diploma in health counselling. I was not committed to learning in my schooldays, but this time, I turned up to each of my classes with an energetic passion to learn. It was such a boost to my self-worth.

Blame and Responsibility

It is common to want to unconsciously blame others, especially when in deep hurt and emotional pain. It is important to become conscious of this and to take *full* responsibility for all your own emotions and your life. This can be tough to do, but if you become the driver of your own life, you will start to take control of that life.

An example of one of the subtle ways we blame is when we are bored and feel uneasy. It can be so easy to become annoyed and irritable with our partner in an unconscious attempt to offset the uneasiness. Just sitting back and looking inwards at how we are feeling not only puts us in control but also helps diminish the tension of this situation.

Thoughts of someone else being responsible for the way you feel can be difficult to let go, thus keeping you stuck in the blaming mode. Having thoughts like *These are my emotions now, and I will feel them and focus on the joy of life* makes this a bit easier. Relationships usually start to flourish with less blame.

Experience

Experience is one of our most inspirational teachers, and being aware of this helps to put more of an emphasis on what is happening to us in the present. You have experienced a lot of life already, so draw on the experiences, and just realise that you have coped many times before.

If a situation is not turning out the way you want it to, just treat it as an opportunity to learn. Of course, change the situation if possible, and make new choices.

You will definitely grow from the experience of a time in crisis, and your life will be that much richer. Learning from an experience of deep emotional pain is one of the best classrooms you will ever attend.

Belief and Faith

One thing I realised as I started to rely more on what others were advising me was that my belief in myself and my faith in my own ability were being slowly eroded away. It became obvious how precious it was to be in control of my life. I started to take more control from then on. I remember a day when I put a CD in the car stereo. There was a song with the words "I'm taking control of my life now, right now." This brought a huge smile to my face, and I laughed and cried all at the same time.

Taking control of my life was a turning point. A turning point can happen at any time if you are aware of just how strong your belief and faith is in your own ability. This is a tool that needs to be sharpened all the time because it can easily be blunted by our thoughts.

Thoughts will always be there; it is just how much attention we give them that can make the difference. Having thoughts of salvation coming from an external source can undermine your self-belief. Following your intuition and your heart will ground you in your own belief and faith.

Acceptance

Giving acceptance to what is happening to you can help stop the urge to panic excessively. If you are overly anxious, your choices will become erratic, so it is important to accept the situation—that is, not to sit back and let things happen but to take firm action with acceptance.

Everything is constantly changing, so trying to control life to be in a certain way is exhausting. You can get into a frustrating fixing mode all the time. Having a certain amount of control in your life is important, but if certain situations are not turning out the way you want, just try to accept them. Acceptance is going with the flow of life and learning. Trying to continually control everything is the opposite.

Gratitude

As I brought more gratitude into my life, I became more and more positive. It was slow at first, but it helped. As I focused on gratitude, I became thankful for everything in my life. I was thankful for all the services available to me—for my family and support, for my coping ability, for the roof over my head, for food to eat, for my next breath. It does not matter what it is; there is always something to be grateful for.

Expression

There are different ways we express ourselves. Some of the more noticeable ones are through speech, body language, and emotions. The way we express ourselves is an indication of our internal condition, and I found it useful to be watchful of how I expressed myself. My self-awareness grew when I realised how words like *should*, *got to*, *have to*, *could have*, or *can't* cause many regrets. I was alarmed at how many times I used these words. Paradoxically, with this realisation I started to make clearer decisions with fewer doubts.

As with all the tools, it is important to not only talk the talk but also to walk the walk. In other words, you need to become more aware of how you express yourself and then make the necessary positive changes. There is always a place we can learn from, but we can stagnate in a spiral of negativity if we are full of regrets. This can build up our fears, causing lack of real emotional growth.

Planning

When I was in the hospital, I saw an advertisement for a free course at a nearby general hospital. I was thrilled when given the permission to attend. Making the decision to do this course was such a positive step for me. It is so important to take opportunities when they come and then follow your instincts.

I found the next six tools that I learned in this course to be of great help when I was still trying to understand what was happening to me. The important thing to remember is to work methodically and initially write things down so that these tools become automatic. Then when situations arise, they can mentally be resolved fairly quickly.

Most of these tools can be used for normal day-to-day living. Planning is a simple tool; you just have to be realistic. Basically, step out your day, and plan long-term and short-term goals. Get out of bed, have a healthy breakfast, exercise, see your friends, and do all the necessary parts of life like cleaning and buying healthy food, going to work, and so on. Write your plans down on paper, and as you do them, tick them off. It might seem such a simple thing to do, but even if you only do it for a short period, you will put planning in the forefront of your mind.

Plan for a holiday, or plan to have that special someone back in your life. I had such a plan, but I needed to accomplish the short-term goals first, so I just devoted all my energies on getting better. I knew from my past that in directing my attention to having someone else fill the emptiness and loneliness I was experiencing was a waste of time and energy.

Problem-Solving

There are set formats to this tool. The main idea is to write down the problem that is making you anxious and depressed and then write down as many solutions as you can. Then go through the solutions, giving them a rating on the advantages and disadvantages, and pick the one with the best rating. It is simple but worked for me.

The thing to remember is that when you have a solution to a problem, you have to be prepared to give it some form of priority in your life. Situations change, so be prepared to adjust your solutions to any problems that arise.

Mood Management

This tool can keep you in touch with how you are feeling and your emotions. As with problem-solving, putting pen to paper will make things clearer. Rate your moods during the day from one to ten, one being very sad and depressed and ten being happy. Then write down what was happening at the time and what you were mainly thinking. You will come up with a pattern as to how certain situations and moods affect your mental state. Some might seem obvious, like your boss yelling at you, and of course there will be uplifting moments as well. There may be other less emotionally charged situations that occur too, but writing all of them down will help you in understanding yourself and your moods.

Negative-Thought Management

One of the main problems with being depressed is the constant negative thoughts that flood your head.

Managing them is essential to your recovery. Write down the main thoughts that get you depressed and then the emotion and feelings they provoke. Then think positively and realistically, and eventually you will see how soul destroying these negative thoughts are. It is up to you then to choose if you really want to keep letting these thoughts control your mental health.

This tool will also help with your daily ritual as you become aware of just how many negative thoughts come into your head. When you start to see the negative aspects of your life, you then have the opportunity to do the work to balance this.

Mindfulness and Focusing

Being in the present, as my therapist, Tom, always said, is the best place to be. If you put your attention on anything *other* than how awful you feel, your focus will begin to change. In doing that, you are becoming more present and not concentrating on the past or what might happen in the future.

I remember one day when I had my first real taste of being present. I had parked my vehicle in a lovely area and planned to just take a pleasant walk. After finishing the walk, I went to the spot where I thought my vehicle was but could not find it. I began to panic and became slightly disorientated. Even after I eventually found it, my thoughts were still racing, so I simply looked at some clouds and focused on them as much as I could. It was not long before I felt calm and at peace.

Focusing on the beauty around you or even simple things like how fast you are walking or how the weather changes throughout the day brings you closer to present-state awareness. Mindfulness is about doing something different to help you become aware of where your thoughts can take you. It is a tool that you can work on constantly to stop mental projections into the feelings of despair and hopelessness. As you do that, you leave room for other feelings, and once you experience that, your focus will move towards all the good in life.

Exercise and Physical Health

Exercise relieves stress, and being in good shape physically gives us a psychological lift. In my circle of friends, many conversations seem to revolve around getting fit. This shows that most people are concerned about staying healthy. The trick is to watch where your thoughts go and try to get fit for yourself—not just for looks or image. A lot of energy is wasted on keeping our image intact, and we can use that energy to just enjoy some form of exercise.

There are many ways to exercise, even gardening is a great way to move the body and you can be creative as well. The important thing is to find what you like doing and, as with all tools, keep at it. I was glad that I pushed myself to get out and exercise because my mood always changed by the time I had finished. It was subtle but enough to motivate me to keep healthy.

One of my jobs was working in a gym as a personal trainer, and I was both frustrated and inspired by some of the clients I trained. The clients that inspired me went on to achieve their goals and more. It was a pleasure to see how committed they were and how they pushed themselves beyond their initial fears.

Could there be a correlation in the fact that sedentary lifestyles are common in affluent countries and depression and anxiety are on the increase? Our fast-paced lives could also be a major contributing factor here, but by simply getting out and moving our bodies, we are giving to ourselves. The more you give to yourself, the better you will feel.

Yoga

Yoga gives you a balance of mind, body, and soul. It gave me a sense of mental and physical control. The poses were challenging for me at first, but as they became easier, I felt the benefits. Stretching helps in the release of toxins that build up with mental stress. Yoga has now become an important part of my exercise regime.

Yoga has a deep philosophy behind it, and you can develop a wonderfully healthy lifestyle by going into that depth. The achievements in yoga are exhilarating, and you can meet some wonderful people in the yoga community as well. It seems to draw people of a kind nature.

Body Awareness

When you are out of tune with yourself, knowing and feeling what is happening to your body is essential to knowing your emotions. Get to know how your body reacts to certain stimuli. Notice things like the heat in your body, your heart rate, your perspiration, your pain level, what your skin feels like, etc. This is a tool that I love to use as it helps me understand how my body is affected by my mental state. I notice the subtle changes that happen throughout the day, and I learn from this experience. I can definitely say that my stomach is a gauge of my emotions.

Body awareness has opened me up to the wonderful benefits of self-healing. I rely more on my own self-healing now as I think there are a lot of illnesses that could be psychosomatic. Through body awareness and with a bit of trial and error, I have found that certain uncomfortable symptoms disappear when I am in a lighter mood. Self-healing has given me a pleasurable boost to my overall well-being.

Healthy Eating

Food is synonymous with emotions and is like a clinical gauge to our moods. When I was feeling low, I stuffed and suppressed my emotions down with food. I say this lightly because food is to be enjoyed, but just being aware of this can stop you putting on weight when you are depressed. If you see this happening, focus on your emotions, and if need be, express them in some way.

There is so much variety of food out there, so try not to restrict yourself to a specific eating plan. Use your imagination to have fun in creating great meals. Healthy eating has been proven to create well-being, and I know it made me feel positive. I am amazed at how much there is to learn about our eating habits and a healthy body.

Group Therapy Programs

There are many groups that can provide you with support and understanding of what you are experiencing. Attending meetings gives you an outlet for all your anxieties. You will get the support you need from caring and compassionate people. Group meeting can be a daunting experience at first but once you begin to connect with people on a similar level you will feel more at ease. Your compassion for others will begin to grow as well as you give them your attention.

A free international organisation that I found to be very helpful was Re-evaluation Co-Counselling (RC). There are very experienced counsellors involved with this organisation who will exchange individual and confidential attention. After learning the fundamentals, you can have one-on-one sessions with people in your area. This is a truly wonderful way to connect with others on a personal level.

As a facilitator for the Isha System I am happy to introduce people to this life changing spiritual practice. It will give you a deeper understanding of your mental and emotional well-being. You will gain the ability to raise your awareness above the normal level of thinking and you will become more confident in your choices. The beautiful part of this practice is that your self-love and appreciation grow naturally.

Giving to Others

Throughout this book I put an importance on giving. In giving, we take the focus from ourselves and direct it to others. To change my focus, I had to be uncompromising in giving to myself. I needed time to face my fears and do the work to become clear in my thinking. Without this clarity, my giving to others was not completely unconditional. By this, I mean that there was a certain amount of compromising and expectations in how I was giving. Compromise can often lead to resentment, so it is important to see this and give unconditionally.

Some people are naturally gifted givers. They have no ulterior motives and do not expect anything in return. They have found how wonderful it is to help others in the act of giving. I came across many who shared their warmth in giving.

Like any positive experience, once you see the gratitude that is expressed from someone you give to, you will want more. I am sure you have been giving in your life already, and just being more conscious of its benefits will help direct where your energies go now.

Self-Pity

Remarkably, there are benefits to depression. People feel sorry for you and rightly so, because this is a horrible time in someone's life, but you have to watch out for the warning signs of feeling self-pity.

Quite often, most of the conversations with other people revolve around you and how you are feeling, and this in turn can become obsessive. I slowly fell into the role of a victim as I felt increasingly sorry for myself. The way I related to people was becoming all about me. Luckily, I saw how people became more and more distant from me and how they just got on with their lives. Showing genuine concern to others and giving them your full attention can reverse the impulse to constantly tell your story.

There are many subtle changes that happen, but becoming more compassionate will change your energy levels. There will always be someone who needs your support and attention, so just be open and share what you have. You have a lot to give.

There is usually an underlying reason for having self-pity, and this will eventually surface as you begin to understand yourself more.

Pride and Dignity

I have often heard the sayings "Pride is the sign of a foolish man" and "Swallow your pride." Pride can get in our way of how we relate to others. There are times, though, when you need pride, especially when you are depressed and you start to isolate yourself. If you combine pride with dignity, your focus will change in how you relate to your environment. Having pride in the way you look and in your surroundings can boost your mood. You do not have to be rich to have nice things around you. Have pride in what you have achieved, and be proud of simple things. Life can be challenging; just be proud of who you are.

Courage and Strength

With this tool, adaptation is the key. As you learn and experience more about mental health, be conscious of how you adapt all of this to your lifestyle. It will take a good deal of courage to change, but as you do, you will gain strength in your mental and emotional approach to different situations.

You need courage, strength, and a willingness to learn all you can about the causes of your emotional pain. Initially, I just wanted to get my life back as quickly as possible. I would often ask my therapist, Tom, how long it was going to take before I felt better. I can laugh at that now, but it is normal to want to be rid of the negative feelings that depression brings.

After a few months, I knew that my depression was not going away, so I became determined to find out more about why I was experiencing the feelings and thoughts I had. I absorbed a lot of new information from different health professionals and my own research. I tried to adapt it to my life, even though I had a wavering determination full of doubt. This was where I needed to be courageous.

The benefit of adapting the information to my perspective was that I developed the internal strength to explore new ways of dealing with my crisis. Courage broke down the fears of the psychological reasoning and understanding that I had absorbed. There was some information that made me more anxious, but this lessened as I grew more confident in how I approached my condition.

Happiness

While there is a strong desire in us all to be happy, it is important to know and understand what will make us happy. Take time to explore this tool. Will money make you happy? Or a friendship? Love or a relationship? Family? The list can go on and on.

I have read many perspectives on happiness, and the main conclusion I've reached is happiness comes from deep within and is better defined as contentment. We can make ourselves happy and contented just by wanting happiness. Being conscious of not trying to find it in anyone else is important as well. A loving partner can give us the support we need, but to overly rely on this undermines the relationship and our own foundation for mental well-being.

I found that getting to know myself and having the courage to explore different ways of becoming mentally stable were giant steps to achieving happiness.

Openness and Friendliness

Opening up yourself will endear you to others. You will be amazed at how they in turn will open up to you. I was terrified at first to say to anybody that I was really struggling to get on top of things. When it became obvious that I was struggling, I let go of the image I was always trying to keep intact and protect. It was a pleasant surprise to see how people responded. There is a lot of empathy, understanding, and compassion out there, and being open is one way of finding it.

We all lead such busy lives with so much to do, and we can get so self-absorbed in ourselves that our openness to each other is sadly diminished. I often thought how sad it was when people did not acknowledge each other when walking along the street. To make myself feel better, I decided to smile at everyone as I walked past them, and I was pleasantly surprised at how many smiled back. It felt wonderful, and I decided to do it more. Simply being friendly and open helped in changing my moods.

Simplicity

We can get bored easily in this modern, hectic life, and quite often we tend to miss the simple things. I suppose you could say it is time to smell the roses. When I began to change, I was excited to see just how easy life could be if I just stepped back and let go of my complicated ways. With little insights like this I began to embrace the beauty of simplicity. In being simple and not complicated, my life became less confusing.

A lot of the tools blend well together, and embracing simplicity can complement many of the others beautifully. The best way to develop a simplistic attitude is in enjoyment. Be conscious of the enjoyment there is all around you; become addicted to the enjoyment of life! It is the best addiction of all, and it is free. It is still important to acknowledge and feel any unpleasant emotions when they arise, but by focusing on the enjoyment you can create a shift in your perspective.

Relaxation

How do we relax? Should we meditate, practice yoga, read a book, go for a bush walk, or go on a holiday? This is a difficult one because we all need to relax when we feel hounded by our outside environment in whatever form it takes in our lives. It could be work, the children, the family, commitments, deadlines, or anything else that causes stress. It is important to realise that no matter what is happening around us, we should always be aware of our emotions. For me this awareness is relaxing.

When on holidays or enjoying some of our favourite pastimes, we can usually spend some time in peaceful relaxation. It is when the holiday is over and we return to work and our normal lifestyles that we find that our peace gets eroded away by the stresses of these lifestyles. In these circumstances, relaxation depends on something external. If our internal state is one of peace, then relaxation is the natural by-product with the pleasurable activities we enjoy having an enhanced value.

To be relaxed and at ease begins with self-awareness. As my awareness grew, I could see where I had always been looking for the next experience of relaxation. I was not fully present with what I was doing at the time. What matters is not *what* we are doing but how we can just enjoy the activity while being as present as we can. You will be pleased as I was of how you can enjoy some of the simple activities that bored you before.

Positivity

Having a positive attitude is obviously a great tool to offset depression. I found that this became automatic when I started getting on top of my lows. Positive thoughts can be used to push out negative ones. Again, I used focusing to let go of the negative thoughts with some good, uplifting, positive thinking. Watching your thinking has so many positive benefits.

There is a balance needed here as well because trying to be too positive can stop you from feeling all your emotions. You can easily suppress unpleasant emotions in trying to be overly positive to keep your image intact.

Feeling emotions is one of my key tools. An example is the ending of a relationship. Rather than push through the hurt and try to feel as positive as possible, you need to embrace the hurtful emotions. A positive attitude can be developed after you have expressed and processed the emotions.

I remember that when a romantic relationship would end, I would just bottle up all the hurt and question myself constantly as to what I did wrong. I did this until the unpleasant emotions eased. It became a pattern of mine, and I thought this was the way to get through relationship break-ups. As I see it now, I was negating the emotions with a thought. The problem was that as I added a thought to the hurt, I was pushing away the beauty of feeling.

When we analyse our emotions without simply feeling them, we do not experience all of what life can bring us. We are not true to ourselves or those around us. Our image gets another layer added to it, and our suffering mounts up on a pile of thoughts.

Going inwards with every opportunity there is to feel has so many benefits. You begin to become real, and this creates such a positive attitude. Being positive can take on a whole new meaning when we are true to every piece of us that needs our attention. Our minds, bodies, and souls blend in a natural expression of life.

Accepting and Giving Love

Giving love comes fairly naturally to most people. Paradoxically, accepting love can be quite difficult for some. A balance can be achieved if you see the places where you think you do not deserve. By *deserve,* I mean the unconscious pattern you have about your own worth as a loving person and what you receive in return.

The love we receive as a child and the way we seek recognition from then on plays a big part here. Being aware of this and understanding this tool will help form a balance in our lives of this most important emotion: love.

Opening up my heart and mind have been the main factors in finding the balance of accepting and giving love, and this has happened quite beautifully and naturally. The resistance I had before of not being able to accept love was the unconscious pattern of the feeling that I did not deserve it. How could I have a balance in my relationships if the love and attention that were given to me were repelled? I had the pattern of unconsciously thinking I did not deserve love, so I pushed it away. What also contributed to this were the thoughts of *What am I doing wrong?*

As with the tool of giving to others, the importance of being unconditional in the way you *give* love will show you how to *accept* love unconditionally as well. Having a balance of accepting and giving love will show in your relationships, and you will receive many pleasant surprises.

Creativity and Imagination

We can all be creative. We can draw, paint, do gardening or landscaping, play a musical instrument, write letters or cards, write poetry, make something, or even cook. Use your imagination to expand your creativity. I was elated at how creative I could be. It was an uplifting experience when I began writing this book. It was very therapeutic and inspired me to try other avenues of my creativity. I started to draw as well. I found that if I just flowed with what I was doing, the drawing took on a realistic scene. A big difference to the unadventurous drawing attempts of my past.

Poetry has also manifested along the way, and when a situation brings up certain emotions, the words just seem to flow. The same happens with song writing. I am able to play some basic chords on the guitar, and there have been times when the music and words came quite naturally.

Having low self-esteem can hold you back in so many ways. It can hide your creativity, so just brainstorm a bit, and do not let the negative thoughts get in the way of you being your true and natural creative self. There is a creative part of you just waiting to shine through.

Moral Awareness

Having good basic morals is a good foundation for healthy living. Morality plays a big part in the way we think, and everyone has been raised in his or her own unique way. This will affect our judgements and awareness. A good set of morals has a certain value. You should simply be aware of how your morals affect your day-to-day living. There can be so many rules that you live by that the enjoyment of life gets squashed.

How strong your morals are and how hard you are on yourself can get confusing. Because of my upbringing I found that I was caught between trying to be myself and being someone stifled by the effects of too many strict religious moral standards. If this is the case for you, try to be aware of this and adjust accordingly so you can have a balance in your life. It is not just a matter of morals, but if you can come away from your judgements of situations and not be hard on yourself, your self-esteem will take an upward turn.

Assertiveness

This is a difficult tool to use, as to be assertive you generally have to be in a fit state of mind. But you have to start somewhere, and it is beneficial to have some form of control of your life. Sort out your wants, and go for them; try to be strong. Being assertive does not mean being forceful and angry; you can be assertive in many subtle ways. Being a quiet achiever in which you just do what needs to be done will help you gain mental muscle.

Medication

This is a difficult one to write about. In my situation I felt that drugs were not right for me, yet I think they can benefit some people for a short period. Medications are not the complete answer to depression; they are temporary helping hands. The main job of healing is done by a natural internal process we all have. Try to be confident and focus on this inbuilt healing mechanism; it is a powerful natural remedy for all your body's pain. Always work with your professional health practitioner when using or going off medication.

There are some herbal, sedative-type medicines available that will take the edge off anxieties and the stresses of everyday life. These are not addictive and will give you a calming effect.

Acupuncture

Similar to herbal medicines, this is a natural way to offset your condition. As with most of the tools, this will give you subtle changes, so being in tune with your body will help in feeling the changes. Any form of natural therapy is beneficial because you are putting attention on yourself. Trying different therapies is a positive step towards healing. Your body is always in a healing process, so having the confidence in this will let the process flow.

Massage

Having a massage is a nice way to pamper yourself. The feel of someone's touch heightens our senses, and it is important to create awareness of every part of us. Massage is just another tool that helps release tension and emotions that have lodged in certain parts of the body. I have found that Thai massages are very effective, as they tend to follow the alignment of the muscle.

Music

Everyone has an affinity with music; it just differs from person to person as to what sounds pleasing. Music can change your mood. Music is so close to our hearts and has such a transformative power. When I was deep into my depression, soothing music made me feel better, but as my moods became brighter, I wanted to up the beat in unison with my upbeat mood. There were songs that were just right for me at the time. Music resonates at a deep level of our consciousness, and it is in that deeper level that we can find peace. That peace can be expanded continually if you commit to a profound daily ritual like the Isha System.

Aromas

This is similar to music. It is personal as to what smells you prefer, but the thing to remember is it is another simple tool that will not cost much. The smell of a beautiful flower can change your mood. There is not much evidence about the efficacy of aroma therapy, but I found that burning pleasant essential oils gave me a calming feeling. Personal experience is always the best evidence of what works for you. Just like other therapies, I think that certain smells have a powerful effect on our health, both physical and mental.

Maintenance

Just like maintaining anything of value, your mental health needs to be constantly maintained. I had a few minor relapses and found that using the tools on a regular basis was the key to not taking my mental well-being for granted. All my tools complement one another, and I am always pleased to see how they blend together. Keeping in tune with your body is so important with the stresses of everyday life. Your body can tell you so many things if you are ready and confident enough to listen to it. It stops that automatic response of seeking help from external sources when we are in physical or mental pain.

Laughter

You forget what it is like to have the basics in your life when you are in a depressive state. One of the simplest basics is laughter. It sounds odd, but when you are deep into your emotional pain, laughing is the last thing you feel like doing.

Laughter offsets many things, especially self-pity. Try to start laughing again. Really laughing—belly-hurting, tears-running-down-your-cheek laughing. You need to be real here and not just laugh everything off, as there are times when you need to express yourself in other ways.

Laughing is a way to keep a brighter attitude because you can quite easily lose the spontaneity of being lighter and just laughing. There are even laughing groups around.

Support

Support from family and friends and, if you are lucky enough, from your partner too is so important. At the same time you cannot abuse this tool. Relying on your support mechanism should be balanced respectfully. This is your experience, and only you will gain the deeper understanding of who you truly can be. If you appreciate your support and take positive steps towards the enjoyment of life, you will find those around you will support you more.

Counselling

Just talking over your problems with someone who can firstly be objective and then give an intelligent opinion is so important to your recovery. As the saying goes,

"A problem shared is a problem halved." The trick is to find the right person. Just be open and honest with the one you choose. If you find yourself stagnating or stuck, tell them how you feel. You will then develop a sound relationship with them, and you can both benefit and grow from that.

Basically, most people have the ability to counsel, but I feel the attributes of warmth and attention are both very important in the counselling process. There were a few people who helped me who had a natural compassion, and I will never forget their warming attention.

Counselling is also important if you decide to go off medication. An understanding of the effect drugs have made on you can help you plan your decisions.

Love and Compassion

We are all on a quest to find love, and it is where we look for this love that is important. How and why we do this can shape our lives. On an emotional vibrational level, love is highest of all, and it has no boundaries. Focusing on love and compassion will change everything about you.

I saw a sign advertising a dating website, and the main heading was about finding your true love. If your search for love is entirely external in the form of another person, at some stage you will experience emptiness. A deeply fulfilling and personal relationship starts when you look internally. It is not that someone else will not fulfil certain needs, but if you find your one true love inside, then the way you love externally will be noticeably sweeter.

With internal true love and appreciation, your compassion will shine more. Your willingness to give what you have is greater because you know you have something of real worth. Also, as you grow in your own confidence, your empathy for others will grow as well. Your understanding of yourself and others is enhanced, and you will want to naturally share that. If your focus is directed towards love and compassion on a regular basis, it will become your normal state.

I am amazed at how I look at people differently now, especially young children. They are so beautiful and innocent. With this perception comes a feeling of unity with others. The more you perceive that, the more you see and experience the innocence and beauty of yourself.

Summary

There are many tools that we develop throughout our lives. By being more aware of them we can use them to our fullest advantage. Through my experience of change and growth I have developed more tools, and there will be more to come in my journey of inner transformation.

The best tools come from our own experiences, and they are catalysts for real change. The changes that happen to you in your quest for peace can often be subtle, but if you stay focused and trust in yourself, you will reap the rewards of your efforts.

My Exercises

The exercises below are ones I used early on, and they all helped. All that I did, no matter how trivial, formed the nucleus of a clearer mind, which brought clearer choices. My exercises were of my own creation, and they released accumulated stress and emotional build-up. In doing this, I was taking more responsibility for my emotions and not taking them out on someone else. Even though my daily spiritual practice has mainly taken over from these, I occasionally use them, and they still work nicely. Anything that works is perfect, even though it might feel embarrassing.

Green Mile

If you have seen the movie *The Green Mile,* you will remember the big guy in jail. As he exorcises Tom Hanks's pain, he opens his mouth and lets out what looks like bugs. I visualise a press in my head and use it to slowly start squeezing out all my fears and negativity. Then as I feel it working, I raise my hands in the air, tilt back my head, tense every muscle in my body, open my mouth, and push out all the fears and negativity at the same time, saying intently, *"No more fear."* Then I come back to the present and look for the good around me.

The Present

Look up at the sky, and hold your hands up. Open them, and look at your palms. Spread your fingers apart, and bring your two little fingers together so they are nearly touching. The gap between your thumb and your little finger on your left hand is your past. The gap between your thumb and little finger on your right hand is your future. The small gap between your little fingers is the present.

Move your thumb and little finger on your left hand together, and do the same on your right hand. The gap in between your hands will open up. This is what we want for our lives—that is, for the present moment to open up for us, because that is all we need. The past has made us who we are, and we can learn from that while not dwelling on it. What the mind conjures up for us for the future may never happen, so it has no real value. It is difficult to let go of our anxieties about the future, but let go of them we must for lasting peace.

Generally, the gaps of past, present, and future change minute by minute, day by day, and week by week, but being aware of the changes is a great exercise to do. We can choose which of the gaps will be the biggest in our lives.

If you look at the gaps for the past and the future as you do this simple exercise, you can see your palms: there is an *end* to these gaps. But as you look at the opening gap for the present; there is no end; just the sky, the universe.

You can do this exercise sitting anywhere, even in company, and if someone asks what you are doing, you can say that you are looking at your life and being present.

Phantom of the Opera

I think of an opera piece, fill my lungs, sing, and really belt it out. At the same time, I visualise all my hurts, fears, and frustrations being expelled as I sing. I deflate and expand my lungs fully in a robust release of emotions. My phantoms are then exorcised. (This also is a great exercise for oxygen uptake to all parts of my body). I then calmly come back to the present and look for the good around me.

Release through Song

I select a favourite song, one with a slow start and a big finish. Usually, my chosen song will generate some form of strong emotion. Music has a special transformative place in our hearts and can make letting emotions flow a lot easier. Whatever emotion comes up is perfect. It means it is waiting there to be expressed. I express my emotions at the end of the song and then calmly come back to the present and look for the good in myself and around me.

All these exercises might seem weird at first, and one of the reasons for this is we tend to keep our emotions suppressed. Any form of release is good. Remember there is no quick fix here; you have to keep at it, and the changes will come. Developing your own exercises is great fun, and having fun is good medicine. One of the main things I want to point out through this guide is to gain confidence in yourself and whatever you do. Always come back to the present after an exercise, stay as calm as you can, and look for the good around you.

An Awakening

I use the word *awakening* as a spiritual term to mean waking up from the old life and venturing into a new way of thinking or a shift in thinking. An awakening can bring many things. One for me was the recognition of the poor ability I had in feeling and expressing emotions. From what I have experienced, an awakening is an opportunity to grow both emotionally and spiritually. For most of us, this comes after a crisis, but initially it is not seen as an opportunity but just pain and suffering.

Every part of us develops from the day we are born. Our personality slowly forms in the natural process of individualism. Situations occur that provoke certain emotions, and our minds start to take control of how we should process the effect this has on us. This process continues with the mind becoming more and more dominant. The innocence we had in our infancy slowly erodes away, and we become separate from the unconditional state of self-love. An awakening is the realisation of just how far we or, more to the truth, our *minds* have become separate from this beautiful innocence. I tend to think that this is what Jesus was pointing to when he said, "Anyone who will not receive the kingdom of God like a little child will never enter it" (Mark 10:15 NIV).

As our lives change, so do our perceptions. Our minds adjust to the changes and try to operate in a controlled manner, which is what we need to a certain point. If we accept all the emotions that arise from any difficult situation and not resist them, an opportunity to grow will manifest. The mind will do the job it has always done and come up with many objections and get in the way of natural emotional expression. If our will to change is strong enough, our hearts will show the way. My awakening is the coming out of the dream of the separation from my innocence, and it is part of my story that I want to share with you.

As stated in my introduction, I had a reasonably normal life until my marriage began to fall apart. After finally letting go of that part of my life, I settled into a new area in a much smaller but comfortable dwelling. Not long after that, I began a new relationship, and life seemed as if it were heading in a positive direction. I even became confident enough to look into an exciting business adventure. My life became fast paced, but it was not long before I started to feel strange. After a few weeks, I decided to do something about it and thought I would be back on track after a short period. I rang a friend after I found out he was a counsellor; his name was Tom. Within five minutes of my first visit to him, he said I was depressed. He introduced me to a lot of new theory and taught me a unique process of how to deal with depression.

The main thing I needed to do first was to accept my condition and not try to resist the painful emotions that kept coming. Once I accepted the pain and truly opened up to it, I noticed slow changes happening. As the internal changes were happening, so were the external. The positive direction that I thought my life was heading gradually took a U-turn. Tom said that there could be more pain and change before I began to understand and think clearly again, and this turned out to be the case.

Learning about what was happening to me was one thing; accepting the reality of the situation was another. Tom said to watch the voice in my head, but this seemed to make me more anxious. There are many approaches to emotional pain, and as I became more confused and anxious, my decision-making became erratic, and I questioned everything I was doing. My self-esteem plummeted, and I listened to anyone with advice.

It soon became obvious to me that my external circumstances were not changing that much, but internally I was changing at warp speed with sadness being my constant companion. I learned about how neural imbalances and the accompanying ruminating thoughts are a major part of the problem, but I could not stop them. At times I felt as if something evil was taking over me. I call it evil because I remember one afternoon when I just gave in to the strange feelings. I eventually had to shake myself though, as I thought I would go mad.

As the confusion and internal changes increased, so did my anxiety. I began to feel out of control, and it became like a drowning circle of uncertainty. I realised I needed to look at other ways to get on top of things. I had resisted the advice about going on medication, but this became a real option.

As my desperation grew, I even contemplated suicide. I was shocked at how easy it was for me to let the thought of suicide come into my mind. It just seemed to come out of nowhere and even made me feel a little stronger. As I stated in the tools, choice can be powerful, and you have to respect its impact.

It was not long before my social life suffered and I lost interest in things that usually excited me. My anxiety and sadness were slowly devouring me. Normally, I would be able to get on top of things, but I just could not stop the downward spiral, no matter how hard I tried.

We all have a certain ability to get through most situations, but this ability had left me. It was a strange feeling, and I began to understand why some people start to lose control and move away from society. I finally decided to see a doctor and go on medication. This ended up being a poor decision. There are a few people that react adversely to certain mood-changing medication, and it looked as if this was the case for me.

After taking the drug, I felt awful and had trouble functioning. I could not work and had to go and stay with my brother. The advice kept coming, and I was told on many occasions that the drug would take a few weeks to work, so I kept taking it. I remember thinking at the time that no one should have to go through this much pain and confusion.

As my confusion increased, I started having trouble sleeping, and this drained me even more. I was prescribed another drug and slowly began to give in to what was happening to me. My motivation and determination were draining away, but still I tried to keep a happy face. Those around me were treating me differently from before, so I knew this mask was not working.

Most of my thoughts were more and more directed at being hard on myself, and it got to the stage where I could not bear to see people smiling or laughing. Being hard on oneself is a common pattern, but mine was becoming excessive. It ripped my heart out to see a family walking down the street. I became so envious of everyone, and this made me more depressed with mounting feelings of isolation.

The thought of my broken marriage made me feel like a failure. These thoughts were echoing how lonely and desperate I felt, and the effects of my strict upbringing added guilt into the mounting despair. I even tried to resurrect my relationship with my ex-wife. I was looking for someone to fix my predicament, but this only compounded my poor decision-making.

It is normal to turn to someone else to find relief from mental anguish, and I was caught in this unworkable pattern. I became desperate for help from some external source. When I ran out of options, I was so confused and anxious that the suicidal thoughts became stronger. I even started to think of ways I could end my life.

I was so tired from lack of sleep and the draining effect of the drugs that basic functioning was difficult. One morning after no sleep and an absolutely terrifying night, my family decided to take me to the hospital. At the hospital I told the doctor about my thoughts, and after an examination, I was admitted and locked into the psychiatric ward. I was exhausted by then and just gave in to what was happening. It wasn't long before I noticed the other people in the ward were experiencing the same anxious state, and it saddened me to see them in such despair. If I had the self-awareness I have now, I would have appreciated the attention I gave these people as I listened to their stories. There is always something to appreciate of ourselves no matter how scared or depressed we get. By giving our attention to others we become less absorbed in our own pain. This can help lift our moods without much effort at all.

After spending time with these people I fell back into the dread of my situation and thought to myself, *How did I end up here?* When a hospital patient talks of self-harm, or even harming others, the staff are obliged to treat the person as a threat to others and take the necessary precautions. I realised I was being a bit too honest with the doctor in what I was telling him and that I had to watch what I said from then on so I could get released from the ward.

Fortunately, the next day my wonderful brother arranged for me to be admitted to a private mental

No Stone Unturned

hospital. The doctor went along with my brother's plan, and I was released from the ward and taken to the private hospital where I stayed for three weeks.

After an examination by a psychiatrist at this hospital I was prescribed more drugs. These had a very different effect on me, making me feel extremely drowsy. After a few days I began to function better, and slowly, my determination came back. I started to exercise and went to all the classes that the hospital staff recommended. Even though I could feel I had a long way to go, I focused on doing all I could to get my life back on track again. All the patients' movements were noted, and I made sure I was making all the right ones.

I can look back now at my time in hospital with fond memories, as there was a camaraderie among the patients. We knew what each other was going through, and friendships formed easily. The only disturbing part of my stay was looking at the amount of mind-bending drugs that were being handed out to some patients. As I started to gain more control, I knew I was not going to go down that path.

In the hospital I felt as if I was becoming just a number. It was at this point that I began to focus more on what my therapist, Tom, had taught me. I listened to my body and put my focus on any emotions that surfaced. The sadness in me was the strongest, and I welcomed it and let the tears flow. It felt natural, and I began to gain clarity with my thoughts. My moods became lighter. It was as if a weight had been lifted from my shoulders. Even though this felt wonderful, I quietly went about my day and tried not to bring attention to myself. I was scared of being diagnosed with another condition.

There was a time while I was still in hospital when I was diagnosed and labelled again. I had read some information about a course at another hospital and asked if I could attend it. I was allowed to go, and near the end of this course I began to laugh and joke with the other attendees. The psychologists that were running the course were concerned about my heightened moods. I was assessed a few days later and became anxious when I was labelled with another diagnosis. The anxiety did not last, as I noticed holes in what the psychiatrist was telling me. This gave my confidence a well-timed boost, and I walked out with more determination than ever to do things my way.

This is when I learned to take control of my own choices. It was a tough lesson but well worth it. It is a lesson I now use constantly. I gained belief in myself and faith in my own ability, and this served me well in my mission to get well. At the hospital I went along with all the advice I was given, and it was not long after that I was allowed to go home. I felt the extremes of all my emotions as I made my way back to my apartment, but I tried to stay focused on the simple enjoyment of being free.

As I tried to settle back into my old life, I realised I had to give myself more time to heal, so I spent most of my days getting stronger physically and mentally. The freedom of just being able to go wherever I wanted was wonderful. I began to plan my days out with all the tools

No Stone Unturned

I had learned. I planned my every move, some of which did not go too well. My past relationships were finished, a business I had started was gone, and I felt so alone, but I had to accept all that and just concentrate on my own worth and abilities.

There were some things that I could not accept, the main one being the drugs I was taking. They were affecting my health, and it looked as if I needed to go on more drugs. I could feel my control slipping away again, and it all came to a head one day when I seemed to give in again to what I can only describe as evil. It is evil generated by the mind, and it can take over quickly. I seemed to just give up after a particularly nasty event, but this day turned out to be a tipping point in my life.

I mentioned in the tools just how powerful our choices can be, and as I fell into the void of feeling nothing again, suicidal thoughts came back, and I made the choice to end it all. I was stunned at how this decision gave me such a feeling of power. The ego and the voice in my head had full control. I had read about the ego and the victim role and the effects they have on us, but I didn't care. I had run out of the energy I needed to survive. One of my thoughts was *I will show them just how sick I am*. It is amazing, but the very thing that is constant in our lives is fear, and all fear comes from the fear of death. Yet here I was ready to do just that—die at my own hands. It was a very strange feeling.

I lined up all the drugs that I thought would do the job, but as I looked at the pills, I realised I could not do it. I tried to pick up the glass I had mixed some of the drugs in, but instead I picked up the phone and rang my daughter. She knew I was in an awful state and simply said, "I don't know what to do anymore, Dad." I began to cry, and after I put the phone down, I made the best decision of my life. I decided to live, and with that, my determination came back. I thought, *If I am going to live, I am going to change.* I have not stopped changing since that day, and I now thrive on change. Pushing my threshold with the awareness of my true nature is one of my main purposes.

Being alone has its advantages, and I had lots of time to plan my life. It was difficult for me to get motivated though, so I wrote down every little step I wanted to do the next day and ticked them off as I did them—simple things like walking outside to get some sunshine, ringing a friend, and writing my thoughts in a diary. They all added up in making me feel more and more alive. It felt like I was creating a new person.

I made bigger plans as well, with the main one being going off the drugs. I planned to do it cold turkey. This is not for everyone, and it went against all the advice both from my family and the professionals. I geared myself up for the day, and I received an added boost to my plans when one morning I woke up feeling very refreshed. I had not felt this way for a long time.

In my planning I would do the same thing every night. I put the sleeping tablet I was taking on the bedside table, and if by eleven o'clock I had not fallen asleep, I would take the pill. The pill would give me about four hours of drug-induced sleep, which was better than none.

When I woke that morning feeling so refreshed and alive, I noticed the sun shining through the window. Normally after taking the pill, I would wake in the dark hours of the morning feeling heavy and just lie there till the sun came up. When I looked towards the bedside table, I noticed the sleeping pill was still there. I realised that I had slept for about seven hours, drug-free. I punched the air and cried with gratitude. This whole experience was truly becoming an awakening.

When the day came closer to stop taking the drugs, I asked the people at my weekly group therapy sessions to think of me. The bond that people share when they are all in such a confused and painful state is truly uplifting. They all showed their concerns but wished me well. This group helped me so much not only as a support network but as an outlet to show my feelings and open up my heart and mind.

As I opened up more, so did my life. It looked as if one of my old relationships that had sadly ended was being resurrected when a person I had missed deeply contacted me. It felt wonderful, but I knew I had to leave it for a while and devote all my energies to making myself happy and not relying on anyone else for this happiness. This was to be another positive and clear choice.

Even though I was feeling anxious about stopping the drugs, when the day arrived, I became quite excited. It was an exhilarating feeling knowing I would be drug-free. The best way I can describe how my body reacted when off drugs was that as the days passed, my heart became lighter and lighter. There were times when it felt as if it would pop out of my chest. I was becoming more confident with my choices, and from then on, my plans grew and grew. I was thankful for the simplest of things, one of the main ones being the wonderful sleeps I was getting. With this experience, I realised that I had not really slept that well most of my life.

Each new day I would wake feeling so clear and full of energy with every day becoming a blessing. Even though I still had more work to do on my emotions and knew there could be relapses, I was just glad to have my next breath. This newfound energy gave me a feeling of confidence and hope. The relapses did come, but as I became more confident and developed more tools, I got on top of things quickly, usually within a few days, with my clarity growing after each relapse.

An awakening is waking up out of the confused state of separation from our childlike, true nature. As adults we have an opportunity to heal this separation by going inward to see where we suffer. In doing this we can shape our own unique stamp on the world. There will always be more to our stories with all the emotions attached. We can add to our stories and gain comfort in the fact that there is always a choice around growing and being more. There is a full and happy life to live if we simply choose to enjoy it.

There are two poems I want to share with you; one was written while in the midst of despair, and the other was my tipping point when my life changed forever. My life tipped towards the reality of who I could be and how I could see the joy of life.

Dreaming

*I dream of days when I can look at the
beauty of a cloud or a flower again,
Of days when my smile and laughter
come from my heart
and I can truly enjoy the company
of my family and friends,
To feel at peace and be happy with my life.
I dream of days when I can tame the
demons in my head because I know
I will not kill them,
Of days when my little brown pill is no longer required,
Of nights when I can dream some more and wake
looking towards what the day might bring.
I dream of a day when I can walk along the
beach with my beautiful grandson,
holding his little hand, playing and laughing with him,
Of days when giving and accepting
love are balances in my life.
I dream of days when sadness only comes and
goes and is not my constant companion,*

*Of days when I can look into the mirror
and be proud of what I see,
Of days when my sensitivity and
strength are of equal parts.
I know these days are possible when love
and compassion flow through my veins
And my heart, soul, and mind are one.
From the help of my loved ones, I know I will
have the strength to make it to these days.*

Findings

*In the midst of a search what do we truly find?
I found depth that I didn't know existed,
and in that, I found an abundance of
love and support.
I found peace.
I am finding a midway where there is a
lessening of comparisons and judgements
and where mysticism and beliefs are rationalised.
I found realisations, not revelations.
I found the emptiness and how
endless the task is to fill it.
I found my openness was returned equally by others.
I found more and more awareness, and this
gave me presence and understanding,*

*and with this understanding came less confusion.
I found that the responsibility for all our
suffering lies in the battle within, and
this enabled less blame, for to blame is to lose that battle.
I found more time where proving isn't a constant.
I found an acceptance to the impermanence of life.
In the act of crying, I found a true and caring
healer to the complexities of my emotions,
and this created clarity, freedom, and more expression.
I found more love and admiration for a person
who guided me to places where fear dominates.
Fear creates many obstacles; with less fear,
I found an ability to change,
A change that can be overwhelming.
In the art of listening and learning,
I found a sameness emerging.
Although suffering has a purpose, this
sameness will transcend the suffering,
And in comfort, through all this, we will all find hope.*

An awakening has changed me to become more spiritually aware in the way I think, express myself, act, and make choices. It has given me inner strength and inner peace, and with inner peace, the rest will follow. As stated in the tools section, I wanted to write on spirituality separately as it has transformed my life in a profound way. Spirituality has a different meaning for each individual person, but it has a common universal aspiration of uncovering the truth in us all.

Spirituality

Our basic makeup includes mind, body, and spirit (or soul), and to me, spirituality means a balance between the three with the spirit shining through more and more. My mind and body have dominated for most of my life, with the spirit silently and patiently waiting for me to let it into my consciousness. I think that the heart and the spirit are deeply connected and that a spiritual journey truly begins when you listen to and follow your heart.

The act of bringing the spirit more into your life is given many names, and the one I like is *coming home*, which means coming home to your true nature, your perfect self. That is far from the unworthy and desperate self I felt when my self-esteem plummeted. I mentioned in "An Awakening" that my "heart felt so light," and this could be another way to explain how spirituality enters into a life. Following your heart is like opening the door to feeling something new, but paradoxically, it is not new. That something has always been there waiting for some form of attention.

Spirituality starts with a search and slowly turns into a way of life. In my search I went back to my religious roots but I found the strictness and rigidity far too restrictive. It did not allow for individuality, and it just did not feel right. I let go of my religious beliefs and started to form what I know now as the one true belief, and that is the belief in yourself. All religions have a deep underlying truth, but there seems to be a misguided belief that salvation lies in the external. Gaining peace and salvation from an external source or somewhere other than this present moment completely overlooks the abundance of our own internal resources and what the present can bring. What is happening right now might not seem as if it will bring peace, but surrendering to it will. Spirituality is about the belief in the deeply personal relationship you develop with your inner being, your inner God.

As I opened up more to this belief, my perspective and perception changed, and I wanted to absorb as much as I could. My trips to the library were both constant and enthusiastic, and the list of books I wanted to read was extended every week. I became grateful to all the great ancient spiritual teachers who had gone before me. Present-day spiritual teachers inspired me with their wise and profound words. This all had a huge impact on me and helped me accelerate along my spiritual journey. They have put ancient, profound teachings into simple, modern, clear language. I truly believe that there is an essential need for a strong spiritual component in our quest for optimum mental health.

My willingness to learn excited me. I even felt an urge to read the Bible, something I thought I would never do as my strict religious upbringing had such a negative effect on me. The words in the Bible began to resonate with me, with the words of Jesus being the strongest. The words I think of when I find life particularly challenging are from the Narrow Gate: "But the gateway to life is very narrow and the road is difficult, and only a few ever find it. (Matthew 7:14 NLT). I would like to think that with this book's help there will be *many* who find it.

My time in crisis was a wonderful teacher. The more I treated it like an opportunity for growth, the more I learned. It brought me love, with the love of others, the love of nature, and the love of myself evolving naturally. Letting go of the voice in my head and listening to the voice of my heart played the main role in giving me fulfilment.

Spirituality has changed many aspects of my life, including awareness and understanding. It has helped raise the level of my consciousness to my thoughts, expressions, and actions. As I travel along my evolving spiritual path, the way I think and express myself continually changes. When I combine this with a more defined meaning and purpose, my passion and excitement for living grows.

Even though at times there seems to be more pain and suffering in this crazy world, I like to think of this time in our human evolution as unique and exciting. Amazing advancements manifest continually and rapidly, and we can universally connect with each other at the press of a button. All that is needed from each individual human experience is the will to learn from the pain and suffering and then share those teachings. I hope you can join me in this enthusiasm.

My old ways taught me;
my new ways guide me.

PART 2

A Spiritual Journey

Passion cuts through the barriers set by the mind.

Introduction

When I emerged out of the dark hole of depression, I was inspired by the creativity that seemed to flow naturally from me, especially poetry. This second part of the book is about the poems and what they mean to me. In this part you will be the witness to my transitional journey from an unconscious condition that was driven by mind-created fear to the conscious state of flowing with life. As with everything we absorb you will create your own meaning from each poem, and that insight is yours to share.

We all have a part of us that is abundantly creative, and to share what is precious is one of the greatest gifts you can give to someone. My poems come from the heart, and it was in listening to my heart that abundance began to flow.

Poems have a timeless quality to them. They penetrate our deeper beings and become part of the emotional whirlpool of our experiences. They are shared in a passionate forum of human inspiration. There is a timeless quality in all of us waiting to be explored in the depth of our beings and our souls.

*Happiness naturally occurs in
the act of unconditional love,
firstly to yourself and then to others.*

Chapter 1

Humble

A journey of suffering is the price to pay
The gift of emotions will light the way
Try to be humble and greatness will birth
Blessed are the meek, for they shall inherit the earth[1]

It has been said that necessity is the mother of evolution. When we find ourselves suffering, it becomes necessary for us to change. It is in that change where evolution takes place. Simply put, we grow more. Our inner selves and emotions are the guiding force in this journey of evolution.

There is a necessity for us all to try to be good human beings, but do we lose our own greatness in our efforts to be good? We can practise humility in this effort, but what does it mean to be humble or to be meek? For me, this means to be strong emotionally, to be in touch with my

---

[1] Last line from Matthew 5:5 ESV.

body with all its sensations and emotions. It means the non-resistance in allowing me to feel everything, even any unpleasant emotions. It means telling my truth and being real with myself and those around me. Most of all to be loving—loving firstly to myself and then to others.

To be humble is not to be timid; it is the opposite. It is to be internally conscious and aware and to take appropriate external action. It means to let go of arrogance and the need to dominate and control by just flowing with life. You can find your greatness in your humility by being your true, natural self with your own unique experience.

A journey of suffering might seem like a high *price to pay*, but if it brings a new perspective, a new experience will follow. There are many different ideas and perspectives from those that I have absorbed, but it is my own perspective and therefore experience that is important. With this in mind, I learned that I had made no mistakes because mistakes are just experiences. When I realised this, I seemed to gain my own power and value. As my perspective kept changing, my faith and trust in what I was doing grew as well.

In my search to grow and be "more", I came across many references to how suffering can lead to positive changes in your life. My interest in everything expanded, and I was like a kid at a candy store. As I walked into a library, I could feel the energy of all this available knowledge and wisdom at my fingertips. Books seemed to jump out at me, and each book seemed to be just what I wanted.

There were many spiritual books and teachers that inspired me, and I wanted to find a practice that suited me. There is a lot out there, and eventually I found one that was simple and did not have a belief structure: the Isha System. There is no right or wrong way to practise the system. This meant I could focus more on my own perspective and step into my power and my own greatness.

The practice can be challenging at times as you learn to listen more to the voice of your heart. The voice in your head or your intellect wants to stay in charge, and this can bring up many fears. These fears need to be felt and expressed, and doing so requires a great deal of trust. As I trusted more in what I was doing, I discovered that *the gift of emotions* was lighting the way.

It is so precious and such a relief to just feel all there is to feel and release all the built-up tension and stress that is accumulated over a lifetime. In my case, not only did I gain emotional stability and strength with this release, but on a physical level, I could feel my body loosening up. I am well past middle age, so this overall experience of self-healing was an inspirational surprise. Along the way my consciousness opened up, and I could see the parts of me that I wanted to change.

There are many ways to define consciousness, and I would just simply say it is an internal ability to focus on what is most important in life in any given moment. For instance, as I am writing these words, my hope is that you find my story honest and can relate to it. That is important to me. Another important aspect of my life is to love and appreciate myself more, and this will happen as my consciousness grows. I am like everyone else, and I want what this earth and life can bring. With self-love and appreciation, I will gain these natural gifts as I *inherit the earth*.

My spiritual growth with all the realisations and changes that I have experienced are embodied in the rest of this book. My consciousness and awareness were the catalyst for the transitional changes that have occurred. They have given me clarity, and this is where my *greatness will birth*.

Chapter 2

Value

There is an immense need for you to be here;
Your ever-changing story is to be told.
To shape it is madness.

If perfection is the acceptance of imperfection,
Then the only real choice is acceptance,
For unfulfilled choices are disappointments.

Our universal heritage is to prove one's worth,
But your value is missed.
The simplest need of all is your experience.

Our value is tested throughout our lives with the effects of our upbringing, our culture and society, and our personal relationships heavily influencing this value. Our stories are all unique, and mostly we tell our stories many times. There came a point in my story and my experience whereby I made a choice just to accept things as they are. My life and who I was did not need to be any other way than what it was; it was perfect. In reaching that point, which I like to call the tipping point, I could see my value. My self-esteem took an upward turn, and my confidence grew. It was such a natural feeling, and I realised I had this value and self-worth inside me all the time. This feeling had been hidden by self-sabotaging, negative thoughts. My true nature became exposed, and my life had meaning.

It is common for people to keep trying to prove themselves. This takes up a lot of energy and that can hinder you from seeing your true value. In trying to prove ourselves we can develop a solid image with strong egoic tendencies. Image is such a strange camouflage that we hide behind. It needs constant attention, and it is draining trying to polish it in the way we relate to everything around us. When our life situations get challenging and our images get dented, we question our existence and sometimes ask ourselves why this is happening.

My image and therefore my story had reached a point that felt unbearable. My energy was drained, and I just wanted to end the story. I believed in and identified with this fantasised story. It is only now I can see what a strange and disturbing decision it is to end one's life. Making the choice to take my life had a real power to it, and I was caught in the unconscious pattern of trying to prove my worth. I thought, *I will show you how much pain I am in and how hurt I feel.* The reality was I did not know how to feel. I was numb, and medication contributed to this. Numbness had formed in me throughout my life because of the underlying fear and resistance I had in feeling all my emotions.

What had influenced my choices in the past was fear. I was often anxious that my decisions would turn into mistakes. I had felt many disappointments around my choices, and this added to the difficulty in decision-making. The fear of making a mistake caused me to suffer in a lot of my choices. *Unfulfilled choices are disappointments*, but we can learn and grow from them. I was too focused on the negative, and my value was being missed constantly.

Following my heart has become such a natural way to break the pattern of suffering. Suffering is a choice. If I feel bad about a decision I make, I choose not to suffer. I feel the emotion and put the decision down to an experience and then choose not to do it again. By trying to get things done the right way, in other words perfectly, I created stress. This hampered my enjoyment of whatever I was doing. To just accept that my choices might not work out the way I thought they would gave me freedom, and freedom *is* perfect. Acceptance is the antidote for our disappointments because *perfection is the acceptance of imperfection*—the imperfections set by the mind.

What does it mean to follow your heart? It almost seems like an airy-fairy way of thinking but that is just the mind's objections. The more I listened to my heart the more my mind came up with doubts and fears. The doubting thoughts caused me to suffer. These thoughts still come at times. They are the little voice in my head;

the heart is the bigger but softer voice. It is not important where this little voice of the mind comes from, but it is important to be aware of it.

The little voice formed around my upbringing, my parents, the harsh environment at the religious school I attended, my relationships and any number of other external influences. I could blame any one of these influences for my suffering but blaming mutes the voice of the heart. The more I take full responsibility for all my suffering the more freedom I gain. Blaming suffocates healing; responsibility regenerates and mends the wounds of our past. I need my mind to live a balanced happy life but I do not need it to take over my life and affect my value. My heart has all the answers; my mind is full of doubts and fears.

To face these fears, I needed to get out of my comfort zone and push myself and grow on all levels. I used to get bored easily by stepping back into a comfortable place, and this frustrated me. Taking what seemed to be an easier option often left me feeling unfulfilled. By going for what I truly want, any option takes on more value, no matter how challenging this option may be. I might get nervous and anxious with the choice of pushing myself, but by not focusing on the outcome of my choices, my expectations dissolve as well. With expectations our *unfulfilled choices are disappointments*, but this is only a result of the boundaries set by my mind.

All our stories need to be told; they are what make us and shape our personalities and how we relate to the world. Our stories are heavily influenced by our upbringings; it is the conscious choices we make after this influence that can make the difference with our existence and our story. In my experience, trying to change my personality is madness because that would be unnatural. It would mean trying to conform and change the perceived expectation of society, but this would suffocate my uniqueness. Seeing the greatness of the person I am is where I can see my value. It is not an arrogant greatness but a conscious awareness of my own possibilities.

When I feel restless and uneasy and boredom sets in, it is important for me to go inward. These are the times when I can evolve more by not sitting back in the stagnation of a comfortable place. Breaking through the restrictions and boundaries set by the mind gave me freedom. I think we all have a desire to break the boundaries and restrictions that we have unknowingly put into place; it is just whether we take action to lessen the impact. Most of us have had the fun and excitement of doing something out of the norm. If we did that more often, normality and conformity might not have such a strong effect on our society. The only thing that would change from then on would be change.

Evolving is inevitable. It is how we evolve that is important. Seeing our value and what differences we can make is becoming a necessity in an increasingly conflicting and violent world. Going inwards and becoming more conscious is where I know I can make a difference. This is where I can find my own value and worth. Relying on approval in whatever I do is something that I can always be aware of now. To rely on approval is like saying, "How do you want me to be?" or "How do you want me to react?" This leaves no room for our value to be revealed.

There is an internal richness in us all that can manifest into our own unique potentials. For me to become richer internally means that what I want to create is always possible. To do this, it is important to be conscious of what I need. I have always created what I needed without being aware of it, and there were many times when I questioned what was happening to me. The fact is I was simply creating it myself. The answer lies in taking full responsibility for all we create, even if it feels difficult to do at the time.

Taking conscious responsibility for whatever I have done and therefore what I have created was difficult at first. Being responsible for everything that happened to me, even if I felt I was justified to defend, enhanced my acts of forgiveness. If I were to take revenge and not forgive, I would not be evolving, and my value may be misplaced. Of course, I speak my truth in certain situations, but it is the internal digestion of emotions surrounding the situation that I do not need to justify. All that is needed is to accept the emotions without judging them. This goes against the way I coped in the past, but the more I do this, the more liberating it becomes. In this way, I do not have to rely on anyone for my internal peace.

Injustice or unfairness is common even if it is a simple childhood game in which one of the children finds that the rules have not gone his or her way. This can invoke deep emotions. I played out this role many times in my childhood. Of course, this seems insignificant compared to people who have suffered injustice on a political, civil, or criminal level and ended up in jail. The injustice is the same, though, and as adults we can draw on those early experiences in order to go inwards and find our peace. Nelson Mandela is an example of how to live with total forgiveness. He just forgave, and in doing that, his value was not missed. In fact, it was greatly enhanced when, in peace, he became the first black president of South Africa.

Suffering injustice has an extremely strong emotion attached to it. The injustice could happen in one of those childhood experiences or in being accused of a crime that you know you did not commit. I can speak on a personal level, as the latter happened to me. I was accused of theft, and the whole process of police investigation left me feeling afraid and helpless. I did not have any control over what was happening, and this gave me a feeling of lost freedom. After the allegations were dropped, I thought I had left the whole nasty situation behind me. It was not until I talked about the false accusation, some years later, that I realised the raw emotions were still there. Freedom was facing these emotions and then making the choice to let go of the surrounding thoughts; otherwise I would stay caught in the internal prison of revenge.

How much of our time and energy do we use when we feel the strong need to justify or defend? This question can be answered only with experience and the amount of suffering or turmoil created by our actions. When we look at the news, there is always somewhere in the world where people think their actions are justified.

When nations use bombing in their justifications, that is revenge, and that creates an enormous amount of suffering. On a personal level I always observe the effects between the fine balance of speaking my truth and the need to be right. If I feel angry and frustrated, I choose actions that will not create any more lingering suffering in the form of revenge. Taking revenge causes anger to fester, and it will not stop until there is the intention of taking personal responsibility for our peace, both internally and externally.

The amount of killing that is committed by those who are convicted and sent to prison is very small compared to the killing caused by wars. It is irresponsible to think that there is justification in this madness, yet it is just accepted. Without any personal responsibility, history keeps repeating itself. It may seem courageous to fight for a cause in battle, but true bravery comes from looking inwards and becoming fully accountable for our own inner and outer peace.

It is understandable how we suppress deep emotions, but the more we suppress them, the more separate we become from our real selves. These emotions cut into the core of our beings and of who we really are. Our outside environment can bring pain and anguish, and the emotions around injustice and unfairness are among the deepest I have felt. With a strong intention of feeling and letting go of all painful emotions, I know I will not be a prisoner to them. This is true freedom, with the only rules being self-accountability. This negates the egoic response to blame or justify.

Another part of the ego or identity is proving your worth, which is a by-product of seeking approval and is such an acceptable part of society. Seeking approval has energy to it, an energy that can be repelled by others. This can leave you with a feeling of low self-esteem, with your value being tested or lost. Being more aware has helped me notice how much I try to prove and talk myself up big to boost my self-image and therefore my value and worth. Before, I would tell my story and experiences with an enthusiasm to offset how I felt. Of course, this was all an unconscious behaviour I had developed. Making it conscious was difficult, but it was part of the change I wanted to make to find my true value. My worth was mainly based on what others thought of me and therefore my story, but this story did not need changing. It was the way I told it that was important.

Creating drama in one's life is another quite common pattern and I think it partly comes from the building up of our stories. In realising I was doing this, the first thing I needed to do was to let go of any judgements I had of myself, as this would destroy my self-worth even further. It was not as if I was stretching the truth when telling my story, but it was the way I tried to prove myself that needed to be looked at and felt on a deep level.

I remember in my teenage years when I started dating, girls would reject me for no apparent reason, and this hurt me deeply. They would have felt my energy of seeking approval and of needing them for my self-worth. Without knowing it, they would repel that energy. This repulsion is an automatic response and should not be taken personally; otherwise our value is questioned repeatedly. As I let go of the need to prove, I can feel the energy of everyone around me change.

In my religious upbringing, I was constantly reminded of my sins and the things that I had done wrong. This is such a negative way to live, and it left me with a lot of guilt. The feeling of guilt hid my true value, and it was so unnecessary. I could never understand why, if I *sinned* so much, God would forgive me. In reality guilt is just a thought provoked by ill-directed teachings. It is an unnatural creation of the human mind.

I was taught to confess and repent for all my sins. This formed a mental image in me of gaining forgiveness and therefore peace from someone else. Forgiveness comes from a conscious choice to be gentle on myself with self-gratitude and appreciation and to love who I am. My worth then has perennial value. We can all be blinded in not seeing this and our own value. You can gain comfort in the fact that *the simplest need of all is your experience.*

Chapter 3

Wake Up Sleeper[2]

Wake up sleeper.
True love has no fear.
Don't be afraid.
We are here.
Wake up sleeper.
The time is here.
Sleep no more.
The world is yours.
Wake up sleeper.
Be bold and be brave.
You have all you need;
Want no more.
Wake up sleeper.
Do not wait to live.
Open your heart,
And all will appear.
Wake up sleeper.

---

[2] Ephesians 5:14 NIV.

> *Suffering can be our guide.*
> *Find the path,*
> *And suffer no more.*
> *Wake up sleeper.*
> *The darkness is over;*
> *The light is here.*
> *You are the light.*

There are certain unexplained experiences that can have a lasting impact on us. They can be strange or weird and seem metaphysical. I call them wake-up experiences. They become part of our stories, and it is how we perceive them that can make a real difference in our lives. In my case, this happened when I started to listen to my heart and let go of the chatter that was going around in my head. When I look back, I realise that in certain times in my life I was not quite ready to follow my heart. My mind was the barrier in making choices that may have seemed too challenging. It was of no consequence to my mind whether these choices were in my best interest or not, so long as it stayed in control.

Some memories of my wake-up experiences have come back to me recently, and I know why I did not respond to them at the time: it was fear, mainly the fear of moving away from my comfortable life. You could say these experiences were the universe giving me something I needed but for which I was not ready. The truth is that my comfortable life was not comfortable at all. The reality was I experienced a continuous internal struggle.

There was a time when deep emotions were surfacing on a regular basis. I would often come home exhausted and just sit crying. Out of desperation, sometimes I would even ask out loud for someone to help me. My cry for help was answered one day when the words *check your emails* seemed to come from somewhere external. In a daze I turned on my computer, and there was an email about an Isha System event. To attend this event meant that I would need to push myself, but with rising doubts and fears, I let this wake-up experience pass.

It was not until about two years later, when I was struggling with intense anxiety again, that the words came back to me. I realised this was the time to fully commit to the practice. This was my first real step in following the voice of my heart. It is challenging to follow this inner voice, and you need to be *bold and brave*. There can be moments when you doubt a new direction. Thankfully for me, that soft voice got stronger. There have been many such moments for me since, but my belief and trust in myself has now transcended the doubts.

Changing my perspective has been such a great benefit. In my younger days, I was never one for reading books, but when I was looking for something more in my life, I borrowed a book on Buddhism. I did not get far into the book because I had trouble comprehending what was written. I was not ready to start on a spiritual path and thought some of the content strange. I remained a sceptic until I followed through with my wake-up calls and started to believe that opening up to all phenomena was essential for personal and spiritual growth.

There are many aspects to focus on when we become motivated by a passion. As I became more committed to changing, my priorities shifted, and I focused on where I directed my attention. I needed to focus inwardly, but putting my attention solely on myself was awkward. My mind came up with excuses and reasons to continue the pattern of proving my worth.

Throughout my life, I often made frustrating attempts in trying to influence others with my stories and opinions. This made me feel wanted and important. Of course, this was an unconscious pattern I had developed. In raising my consciousness I could see how this made me feel superior. This feeling had a temporary effect, and I would need to keep telling my stories with an exaggerated enthusiasm. The other problem, as I learned later, was that it annoyed people.

Other aspects of where my attention and focus went were minor but still needed changing. To change I just needed another jolt or wake-up call to really start to follow my heart. The jolt came when my physical health suffered. I had been healthy all my life, and my declining state created overwhelming stress and anxiety. After nearly two years I eventually regained my health, and the wonderful part about this period was that I began to trust and believe in myself and my own healing abilities. I became committed to changing, and my spiritual practice was part of that commitment.

To fully commit to this practice I wanted to spend an extended period of time at one of its centres. The Isha System has a six-month advanced program that you can attend at its main centre in Uruguay, South America. At the centre, you get an enormously compassionate group of teachers that are dedicated to help and support you as you clear your emotional debris and raise your level of consciousness. It is a program where you face your fears and challenge yourself to change and grow. It was extremely difficult to leave my family for this time. Change can be like that, but when your heart calls loud enough, you have to follow it. The Spanish word for change is *cambio*, so I called these six months of my life *the cambio*.

Having a loving family around you is wonderful, and I devoted a lot of time to my family. My cambio was a time where I could put all my energies, my focus, and my attention on myself. It was a time to save myself and not others. It is common to develop a need to save others whereby you project your fears onto those closest to you. This need in me had become very strong indeed. When someone else is experiencing difficulties and is in a hole, it is not a good idea to jump in the hole with them. The opposite of this is simply expressed in the saying that if you heal yourself, you can heal the world.

After I returned home from my cambio, I felt that same need pulling me again. This is natural when you have been away such a long time. This meant there were further aspects I needed to heal to wake up more. It was essential in doing this to focus on the tools I learned in my cambio.

As I became more conscious, there were other experiences that were a bit weird and some that were beautiful. One morning I woke in an absolute panic. The panic subsided when beautiful Irish music filled my head, followed by the words *welcome home*. I fell into a wonderfully peaceful and calm state. This experience had a deep effect on me, and I wrote a song with the tune of the Irish music. I would sing it to my grandson, and he loved to hear it.

Other experiences came without the need for the strong inner voice to jolt me into action. My inner voice became a natural part of me, and I felt more at ease in following its direction. To take this leap of faith can seem challenging, but it sets you free from domination of the mind and the fear this brings. The more I experienced the life I wanted to live, the more I was willing to follow where my heart was trying to guide me.

Experience is our best teacher. With this as our focus, we can change the feelings of regret, when we feel we have made a mistake, into an opportunistic experience of learning. With this new perception, mistakes transform into a place of growth. It is like looking through a clean window and seeing that things on the other side are not quite what we thought. As I cleaned the window of my mind of the built-up grime produced by my thoughts, what I perceived as too hard became easy, and life flowed. The grime was the stress I accumulated over a lifetime. It was stress that had obscured and clouded the truth.

The exciting science of quantum physics has shown and proven that our reality is not quite how we perceive it. Apparently, scientists can prove this but cannot quite understand it. They have touched on something that is embedded in Eastern philosophy: we are one with everything. Understanding this can become too clinical when all that is needed is an experiential trust and belief in ourselves. As I trust in what I am doing, my perception changes naturally. The desire to gain more knowledge and understanding has gradually diminished as I focus more on what my own experience teaches me.

Suffering can be our guide if we take the opportunity to change when it occurs in our lives. It can come with the sadness of a loss or simply from an emotion that gets activated from a hostile comment. The response we have to our suffering can be automatic. It is said that suffering is addictive, which assumes there is a craving for it. I view it more as an inheritance that has been passed from one generation to another. It is an inheritance we can learn from. There are tragic situations that are the obvious cause of suffering. The learning can come from any internal suffering that lingers and the choice we make to end it. Certain situations are out of our control, but what happens internally is not. If our goal is to *suffer no more,* our internal suffering can show us the path to peace and this can be an inspiring inheritance we can pass on.

Our behavioural patterns are a form of inheritance. A pattern that was played out in my family was angry outbursts of rage. I was exposed to this from an early age, and I kept this pattern continuing in my own family. After an outburst involving my young son, I vowed never to show this rage again. I felt relieved to stop this pattern, but in doing this, another pattern emerged. In pledging not to show my anger again I was labelling it.

For me, labelling any emotion generated fear, causing me to suppress the emotion, and I kept the vicious circle of suffering going. Of course, this was an unconscious pattern; becoming aware of it was liberating. It required constant vigilant attention to my thoughts, which only made the emotions seem worse. Thoughts are just thoughts, but when they are projected into the future, suffering occurs.

Negating or suppressing emotions has a limited lifespan, and eventually suffering occurs in the form of confusion, depression, anxiety, and even illness. I thought I was being righteous when I vowed to stop exploding in anger, but this caused a frustrating internal turmoil. I tried many ways to relieve this frustration. I was involved with different types of groups, and they all had their own unique healing process. Some were strange at first, but I was willing to do whatever it took. It was like walking down the unknown path of what works and what does not. To *find the path* meant to finally believe and trust in what felt right. The spiritual practice I chose was perfect, as it did not have a religious belief structure, and it blended perfectly with my lifestyle and philosophy.

Being grounded and stable in my consciousness has given me the feeling that there is no need for any more wake-up calls. There might be more to come, but I feel at ease knowing the path I have taken will guide me in every moment to *suffer no more*. The wake-up experiences I had before came from an internal place and not from an external source. My wake-up experiences were the

God in me that brought me closer to my own truth. "God made man in his own image"(Genisis1:27 NKJV) and "God is love" (1 John 4:8 NIV); therefore, I am that love and that truth.

There is less need for me to find love externally. Internal love is a true love. To be anchored in internal love means to be unafraid of your own greatness. It means to *be bold and be brave* as this greatness unfolds in you. This gives you the experience of a newer perception in which you see that love is all you need. This new perception also shows you that you have unlimited potential and that *the world is yours*. I now realise that the pain and suffering that come with life are just like a game. It is a game that can help you grow, a game that can guide you to appreciate more and take full responsibility for everything internal. Internal love can bring you into the light and help you realise that *you are the light* of all you create.

Chapter 4

Life

Life can be as short as your next breath
With confusion and the dominance of fear.
Life can be as long as a rainbow
With beauty and no end.
Take a deep breath, and follow the rainbow.

My daughter's life turned upside down when she got the horrible news that a lump in her breast was cancerous. The relationship that we share is very special, and the thought of seeing her go through so much fear and pain deeply affected me. It is natural to become strongly attached to a child, and that attachment feels like a part of you. Like any strong attachment we cling to, we can become overly obsessed with losing it. Initially this was this case for me.

The situation created confusion and an internal fight inside me. The confusion cleared when one day I just cried and cried for my daughter and felt both the fear and sadness for her illness. The sadness was obvious, but what was not so obvious was the projection of my fears towards losing her. All I needed to do was just feel and be open with her and share my emotions. By doing that, I could let go of my fears and therefore my attachment to our relationship and could just enjoy life as it was. I am pleased to say that she recovered well from all the drugs and radiation therapy, and the cancer has not returned.

In the midst of a dilemma there are some people that exude the attributes of compassion and kindness in caring and philanthropic ways. I was touched to see this happen with my daughter's dilemma. She was told she needed to take an expensive drug, and a week or so later she received a cheque in the mail for the cost of the drug. I was deeply touched by this, and I wanted to thank whoever had sent it. After making a few phone calls I eventually had my calls returned. I arranged a meeting, and my daughter was excited to come along too. At the meeting I learned that this person's friend had died from breast cancer. Before dying, one of her wishes was to help ladies, in any way possible, in their struggle with the disease.

In meeting this wonderful person, I was shocked to find that she was suffering from a debilitating disease. She was able to push her fears aside and work passionately and unconditionally for the foundation. She put her heart and soul in supporting women in adjusting to the distress that the diagnosis of breast cancer can bring. It touched me so much, meeting this lovely person, that I went about organising a fundraising day. The day turned out to be one of those special days that you never forget.

When a life-threatening disease is thrust upon a family, life takes on a whole new meaning, even if it is only briefly. It has always inspired me when I see how very sick people change their focus to how precious life can be. They seem to be able to naturally let go of the fear that surrounds their circumstances, and they radiate peace. Even sick small children seem to grow in their wisdom, and that is beautiful to see. They give you something of themselves in this beauty.

Giving is such a beautiful way to not only connect with another human being but also grow internally. If there is an unconscious expectation in the form of a reward when we give, we are attaching a condition to the giving. The reward could be a certain type of response or even approval. In essence this is a subtle form of taking. When I became aware of the expectations I had when I gave, I was both surprised and relieved. It meant there was another part of me that I could change and grow. Certain patterns can be hard to detect, and it was a relief to clearly see how this pattern had affected my relationships in the past.

After surviving any crisis you begin to realise just how precious life is. Just to take your next breath can be appreciated. *Life can be as short as your next breath*, and it can end in an instant. Appreciating everything we have helps us to let go of the things that cause us conflict and suffering.

In some spiritual practices, focusing on breathing is a major component in the growth of consciousness. Becoming conscious of each breath puts you in the present state of awareness where the past and future have less impact. It seems such a simple action, but focusing on and appreciating the simple things in life can cut through the *confusion and dominance of fear* that come when our lives get turned upside down. The fear loses its dominance, and something new enters our beings.

Creating something new can give us a renewed vibrancy and energy. Mostly, our thoughts govern where our energies are directed. If my thoughts form into self-destructive patterns that sap my energies, my moments of clarity diminish. Clarity is an antidote when fear strikes unexpectedly. I experienced this one morning when I awoke with some confusing thoughts. The thoughts shocked me, and as my fear mounted, the clear words *feel; don't think* entered my head, and my fear slowly faded. They are simple words that mean so much. It is not so much the thoughts that always come but how they interfere with the simple process of just feeling. The Holy Grail of a spiritual practice is to enter a place of silence or stillness. Not letting thoughts get in the way of feeling puts your hand that little bit closer to that Holy Grail. This was a new experience that gave me a lighter and less fearful look at life.

There are many wonderful books written by clear spiritual teachers. Their words resonate with me, and I know I am just touching the surface of what they perceive as true reality and not the false reality of a fear-driven life. As my perception keeps changing, my energies are conserved and directed to the things I want and need in life. Where I use and put my energies depends mostly on my thoughts, so giving my negative thoughts less power gives a greater chance of these things manifesting.

Any task can create an internal battle of trying to prove ourselves. I was caught many times when whatever I was trying to achieve became like a frustrating chore. Having the conscious ability to see this allows me to let unproductive thoughts pass and to devote my energy and clarity into creativity, and that is liberating. This also has given me the added benefit of simply focusing on enjoyment and achieving from the heart.

Another example of where I direct my thoughts and therefore my energies is my physical health. My body sensations are a way to gauge the effects of my emotions on a physical level. I want my life to *be as long as a rainbow*, and on the physical plane, this is definitely possible. On an emotional and mental level, I am experiencing life, metaphorically speaking, *as long as a rainbow, with beauty and no end*. It is the beauty and not the fear that gives life an emotional longevity. Appreciating life in all its ups and downs will give it a *beauty and no end*. Having more energy can add to the beauty.

Some of my thoughts can be quite ugly, and this can deplete my energy. Minor situations can provoke an automatic response, and my energies can change immediately. What is important is where my focus and attention is directed. Letting such thoughts go really does give life *a beauty and no end* to what I can achieve. Without the negative thoughts affecting me, I take more control as the director of my mental movies. The negative thoughts will always be there by the thousands; it is just that their power is diminished.

Just like the pot of gold at the end of a rainbow, so too is the potential in what I can create. A rainbow has a natural beauty and shape, and I would like for my life to be connected to and mirror that beauty. The shape of my life is then a naturally created extension of my authentic self and not one that needs approval or has a reliance on achievements. My potential flows into everything I do.

The colours of a rainbow fascinate me, and I never get tired of gazing at their beauty. Out of nowhere come the beautiful colours. Our beauty can come out of nowhere as well. The beauty has many forms, and we all feel its presence from time to time. Coming home to our own beauty and wisdom can be a conscious choice. The *confusion and the dominance of fear* can be the catalyst in making this choice.

When my daughter's hair started to fall out from the effects of chemotherapy, I thought she would lose her beauty. When I arrived at her place one day, I could see how her skin colour had changed. She looked very sick with dark circles under her eyes, and she had a cap on. I could see that she had shaved her head. When she removed the cap, I saw a strong and determined young woman standing there in her beauty in spite of her illness. I talked about this in my cambio, and I cried when the person I was expressing this to said, "Mirror, mirror." This meant what I saw in my daughter that day was my own beauty, strength, and determination.

We all mirror one another, especially our parents. Whether we agree with or reject this concept is up to the individual. Knowing this and seeing the truth in it is wonderful but at the same time a bit depressing. We may not want to accept this when we see things in people we do not like. The frustrating parts we see in others that are annoying or even make us angry can be what we need to look inwardly at on some level.

When we consciously become aware of our mirrors, there is an acceptance and a need to take a lighter look at this; otherwise, our mirrors will show us what we do not want to see. With an acceptance and a lighter perspective, the mirror can be polished on a regular basis. Our judgements and criticisms will then fall away as we realise we are all one and the same. In healing this separation of others, we heal the separation from our true nature.

I think Jesus was referring to the mirror when he said, "Why do you see the speck that is in your brother's eye, but do not notice the log that is in your own eye?" (Matthew 7:3 ESV). These simple yet profound words can be taken out of context. It can be hard to accept that the annoying traits in another person could be a part of us as well. We may have a tendency to be hard on ourselves, causing a feeling of low self-esteem. The answer is to have a loving acceptance of who you are because you are willing to make the internal space for change. Of course, there are always the wonderful qualities of others that we find beauty in, and that is part of the log we can see as well.

There were many aspects of my religious upbringing that caused me to be hard on myself. My main focus was often unconsciously directed to what I was doing wrong. I felt as if I were sinning on a regular basis. The word *sin* means to miss the mark or miss the point. I perceive this as meaning we are sinning when we are caught in the grip of suffering and not realising our own true nature and inner beauty. If I were to rely solely on the religious teachings I was exposed to, and not on self-belief, I would not have seen this. The belief of these embedded teachings was that salvation came from an external source and that you had to obey a strict set of rules to obtain this salvation. If you did not, you were a sinner. I think there is an essential need for those affected by such dogmatic influences to find inner beauty for themselves. With an emphasis on finding internal beauty through self-belief and not on how much we sin, we can come closer to hitting the mark.

Jesus could see his own internal beauty, and I am sure he wanted us to see that in ourselves. It can be as simple as looking inside and letting go of all the thoughts that obstruct us from seeing our own beauty and the beauty that is all around us. Aiming at the connection and oneness we have with everything is a pattern we could embed in our beings. The mark or beauty would be everywhere. The uplifting feelings we have when we see a rainbow gives us a glimpse into what we could all aim for. All that is needed then is for us all to *take a deep breath and follow the rainbow.*

Chapter 5

Harvest

Hearts broken open,
Raw feelings exposed.
With landscape changes
The seedlings will grow.

Ready the soil;
Plough your mind.
With hearts broken open
The harvest will show.

On any spiritual journey, seeing how much you have changed can be difficult to gauge. My expectations on how this journey should be caused me to suffer. Looking for results was my main focus, and I envisaged being in a wonderful peaceful state all the time. The peace does happen, but I do not use it as the only gauge. I have learned to let go of any expectations and simply expect the unexpected.

Life presents itself in many surprising ways, and my peace will come and go. My attention can be drawn away by the dramas that are continually occurring around me. The dramas will always pull at me, and my peace depends on where I put my focus. It requires my constant vigilant attention to see what I am focusing on in each moment. I could be feeling sad or happy at any given moment, and they both require my attention. If I push the sadness away, that is just an old behavioural pattern, and I know from experience this sadness will return even stronger at some point. In changing my old patterns I was reinforcing my new knowledge, and this was another leap forward in my path to freedom.

Learning new patterns means unlearning certain behaviours and our reactions to situations. There is an adventurous quality of learning something different. Being aware of how the mind can create opposition to this will make the learning more enjoyable. It is only the mind that makes it feel uncomfortable when we are on an inner adventure. As the results begin to come, those feelings soon disappear.

There are many gauges and experiences that show us how far we have journeyed on our quest to be free of our mind. Appreciation is one that can be focused on constantly. How we show and feel our appreciation will determine the level of our *peace meter*. If we dwell too long and too much in our suffering, that meter will show empty, but if we are willing to focus on appreciation on a regular basis, the meter will register full.

Every journey is always experiential—no one can take the journey for you—and it is important to see the progress that you make. Just as a farmer knows what to do when he sees the growth of a crop, we too can know what to do in our spiritual harvests. It can be a slow, frustrating process at times, but it is well worth the work. If you have ever planted a seed and watched it grow, you will appreciate the pleasant feeling this gives. Your internal growth and maturity will give you an appreciation far greater.

My experiences are the gauge of what rewards I will reap. Initially my progress was hardly noticeable, and this was where trusting was essential. Trusting envelopes any doubts and frustration we experience on a spiritual journey. Pushing what I used to perceive as boundaries has shown me there is no limit to the rewards of inner transformation. This gives me the inspiration to stay focused and riveted in the trust of what I am doing, even when there are signs that my growth seems to have plateaued. The easiest way to offset these signs is by simply enjoying whatever I am engaged in and by not focusing on the outcome. It could be as simple as having a conversation with a friend where I try to give my unconditional attention. Focusing on the outcome of what you are doing is taking. To simply give unconditionally is a sure sign that you are progressing on your journey.

As I was growing up, I went through the usual personal relationships, and there were times when I was hurt and my heart was *broken open*. The problem was I was not open and vulnerable enough in expressing how I felt. Numbing out the pain of being hurt was just part of the way my mind was trying to stay in control, but that got in the way of true feelings. Showing emotions is the way to enhance a relationship, even when your heart feels broken. To feel everything and change is true growth.

Just like seedlings need energy to grow, so does our own internal growth and maturity. This energy flows from the abundant internal resource of love. We just need to dig deep and clear some of the rubble before the love will manifest. As my energy changed, I noticed different responses from those around me. It became like a magnetic attraction rather than the deflating rejections of my past.

Our hearts can seem as if they are broken open whenever our romantic gestures are rejected. We have all lost in the love game at times with our *raw feelings* being exposed. One of my first experiences of this was when my third-grade teacher gave me special care when I had a toothache. This attention and the feelings I had towards her were new to me. I felt both touched by her attention and sad at the same time. These are the same feelings I have now at certain times. They are part of me, and there is no need to label them. To feel all these emotions is to love, and even though my heart feels broken open at times, I prefer to have that experience than to feel nothing and therefore go through life with a rock-solid heart.

Love affects many aspects of our lives. It is such a strong emotion and is responsible for a vast array of choices and actions we make in its name. It can make us explode in a fit of rage or crumble in the depth of despair. At its most brilliant best it can grow and blossom, giving us a wondrous taste of pure delight. It is like a seed full of energy that has been planted in each and every one of us. When we look for love only externally, the seed will stay dormant. I looked for love only externally, and it always ended the same way. I seemed to fall easily into a victim role, and this intensified the hurt of being rejected.

I read about the theory of giving, receiving, and deserving love, but by only intellectualising it I was just touching the surface of my inner *landscape*. There needed to be some deep internal *landscape changes,* and I was prepared to do whatever it took. My need to find a balance in giving and receiving love became strong, and it always amazed me how I stayed committed to changing. When the heart calls loud enough, it becomes a powerful force.

Whenever my heart was *broken open*, I fell into the depths of negativity. I wondered what was wrong with me and why I was being rejected. This brought with it confusion and the *raw feelings* of low self-esteem. Without making any internal changes, this scenario kept happening, and I would just accept it and even expect it from those I was seeking love from. This defined my worth and affected how my relationships turned out. I would compromise to fit to the person I thought I should be.

When you want to see how much you have grown in any area of your life, you can often be influenced by outside opinion and approval. To truly grow and find the balance between giving and receiving love, I let go of my reliance on recognition. It is understandable when we look for recognition and responses from the outside, especially where love is concerned. The deep connection and relationships we had with our mothers from birth were ones full of interactive responses. This first love sets in place the need for external responses in the role we play out in the love game.

In realising I had to find this love internally, I was not sure how to go about it, and my mind became like an opposition in a battle. I had read that no one else can make you happy, and my mind would come up with a response like "but they can sure make you feel wanted." To feel wanted meant that the other person's reactions were crucial to how I felt about myself. The more I witnessed the objections from my mind in finding internal love, the more I looked to my heart for the answers. The heart can show you how great you are without any outside influences.

Greatness may seem as if it comes from an image of who you are, but it is the exact opposite. Greatness comes from the heart; greatness grows as the desire to love and be compassionate and "give" becomes stronger. Giving is expressed beautifully in the saying "Give and you shall receive." I like to add another word to it, and that is *unconditionally*. Having no unconscious desire to receive something in return for your giving means that the way you give is unconditional. It is a good idea to be vigilant in watching where your giving is not quite as unconditional as you thought. This applies especially to our personal relationships when the expectations of being loved are not met.

There is always a place where you can give. By firstly giving to yourself, you will not be caught in a perpetual state of compromise. My dear mother gave so much in her life; the only thing that was missing was giving to herself. Her life was full of compromises, and she fell short of self-giving. She was at turmoil with herself, and in her later years, I sensed her frustrations and resentments. You may feel wanted whenever you give, but someone else needs to be dependent on you to keep this feeling alive. You can easily lose your zest for life if there is no one relying on you anymore.

Giving yourself the praise and love that you deserve, without any conditions, is a worthy objective. If my mother had given this to herself, her perspective would have been different, and she would not have been so hard on herself. I saw these same patterns in me as well, and as I started giving to myself, love and appreciation grew. This extended into everything, and I became grateful for simple things.

Self-giving is not a selfish thing to do, because it transforms the way you give. If you focus on appreciation, your perspective changes, and if you share that with others, you are then giving to them as well. This has meaningful value because you are sharing your joy of life, your inner harvest. You are changing the landscape of your internal structure, and sharing is your indicator of growth.

Like any form of cultivation, you need a good base or foundation; otherwise, growth will be very poor. This internal foundation, or your authentic self, is always in place. Uncovering this foundation for growth is both an unlearning and a learning process. The unlearning is the clearing of the old ways that have left a field of weeds and rubble that cover the real you. This is exposed as you *plough your mind* to find a new way of thinking. The weeds and rubble of your past use up unnecessary energy and hinder your state of presence. The past or future will not give you the rich harvest of peace; the present moment will.

Staying focused on the present, especially when emotions like sadness surface, can be difficult. My old way created confusion and even annoyance when I felt sad. Mostly, I would just suppress the sadness, but this left me in a limbo-like, numb state in which my confusion became worse. I was unconsciously and automatically resisting the emotion.

A limbo-like state is like being in no-man's land where the soil is barren and infertile and the chance of a harvest is nil. One of the sweetest crops you could ever harvest is love, and it is where we sow the seed of love that is important. I needed to sow this seed in a rich and vibrant place that could sustain growth forever.

I have had many subtle glimpses into the adverse effects of my inherited old ways or patterns. To see the underlying cause of these patterns was such a relief. The way I became angry and annoyed at simple things was frustrating, and this only added to the anger. The subtle glimpse was to find that lying under the anger was sadness. Sadness has a certain blameless element to it and that adds to its beauty. Once I saw the beauty in expressing how sad I felt, my resistance to feeling it diminished. Feeling is such a natural part of life, in resisting, I was fighting against life.

Going deeper into our emotions, especially sadness, helps to soften the hardened image we portray to others. This mental image is responsible for how embarrassment plays out in our lives and is the false sense of who we are hidden behind its facade.

We create what we need, and creating drama in certain situations seems like an acceptable part of people's lives. How the attraction of movies or soap operas plays out in our lives points towards this. The biggest drama that has ever been told is looking for the person that will bring you love and happiness. I was no exception. I needed someone to fill the emptiness of the love I did not have internally. The only true source of love and happiness is found by going inward.

Love affairs happen quickly, and we can fall in love instantly. Internal love affairs happen slowly and keep evolving. It is an affair that needs to be constantly cultivated with self-appreciation so as not to stagnate. It can then be harvested, and with a grounded conscious foundation, it can flourish. The genesis of self-love is self-appreciation.

The mind or the intellect is such a powerhouse. It is like a persistent weed, and it will just keep trying to invade and take over. These mental weeds need to be cleared and ploughed to see the mind's strong resistance to change. The mind will try to keep you stuck in life's dramas where love is not realised in the romantic scenarios the mind creates.

There is an infinite potential in everything—even weeds sprout beautiful flowers. The mind has an infinite potential, but with its limiting thoughts, it can hinder our growth. Life can become like an unwinnable internal battle if we let these thoughts take hold. The battle is won when the thoughts become a friend and not a foe. The thoughts lose their power in this peaceful surrender.

In the modern world growth is measured by the amount of material wealth that is accumulated. On a personal, national, or international level this takes the form of possessions and their magnetic attachment. Internal wealth does not attach; it is just an experience that is preserved in our evolution towards the harvest of inner peace. We all deserve a beautiful harvest, and it always waiting silently to be reaped. When you are ready to *plough your mind* and push through the thresholds you have created *the harvest will show.*

Chapter 6

Rest

Give me peace; give me rest.
Let the veil of calm enter my soul.
Take me to the place of dreams
And not let evil persist.

Nothing is secure,
And there will be more pain,
But there will be rest—
Sweet, blissful rest.

Breaking the backbone of my fears,
I give thanks for a new day.
I give thanks for the peace.
I give thanks again and again and again.

We all have had the experience of waking from a deep sleep feeling refreshed and clear. When I experienced that period of truly restful sleeps whilst emerging from my time in depression, I appreciated how much more energy I had throughout the day. My batteries were fully charged, and I felt ready for whatever the day would bring me. It was such a change from the low energy and the dread of being depressed when I would wake feeling so drained. Re-energising through rest is vital for a vibrant life. Rest can result not only from the reliance on the sleeping state of altered consciousness but also from the peace we experience throughout the day in the state of awakened consciousness. The mind is the barrier that invades this experience, and to realise that its dominance or control is the breeding ground of our doubts and fears is freedom. Without this knowing the mind can cause the merry-go-round of suffering to spin constantly.

It seemed strange to me that my mind created so many fear-driven thoughts when what I really wanted was to be free of my anxieties and to *let the veil of calm enter my soul*. It was as if I had a split personality; one good and one evil. I think there is a nurturing part of our beings that has a subtle way of protecting us from the control of our minds. It is that part that brings freedom. All that is needed is to listen to it. The catalyst that helped me to listen was when I'd had enough of lying awake at night with all the bombarding and ruminating thoughts that caused me to suffer. The experience of restful and peaceful sleeps reinforced the awareness to this subtle part of my soul.

One of the cornerstones of Buddhism is the four noble truths. Basically these truths direct followers on a path to end their suffering. In his clarity, the Buddha gave his insights in simplistic ways. When he reached enlightenment and the end of fear, he wanted everyone to experience this as well. With this simple approach, I ask myself when making decisions, "Will this cause me to suffer?" If there are external circumstances out of my control, I bring acceptance into the picture. With ancient wisdom like Buddha's as an inspiration, my goal is to move towards ending my suffering by *breaking the backbone of my fears*.

Stress and suffering are an inevitable part of life. In resisting the simple and natural experience of feeling, you can turn emotions into an enemy, and this is suffering. "What you resist persists," by unconsciously resisting certain emotions, I was letting an evil part of me dominate. It is not that I am an evil person, but the confusion this creates is evil.

In Matthew 5:39 (KJV), Jesus said, "Resist not evil," and this is often used in the context of forgiving. I take it further to mean the internal battle that was created by my disturbing thoughts and their corresponding emotions. The thoughts would produce emotions that I resisted as my upbringing had me believing that certain thoughts were impure and evil. In not giving these thoughts any power and just accepting them, I was releasing the guilt of a strict upbringing. Without guilt I could focus more on the good in me. Guilt has no substance; it is a man-made fabrication.

Suffering was evil when I was caught in its grip, and I longed for peace and calm. In letting go of my resistance, I started to feel a natural happiness. The evil or suffering started diminishing, and there were times when it felt like a *veil of calm* entered my soul. There was lightness to how I felt. It is this lightness that pervades the complicated state of seriousness. A life that is full of seriousness is a life of suffering.

As I tried to cling to those feelings of calm I soon realised this would cause only more anxiety. I was scared I would slip back into the evil suffering mode, but I was not flowing with the impermanence of life. I just surrendered to this and became more committed to the changes that would give me more acceptance of my fluctuating external environment. In accepting the impermanence of life and the fact that nothing stays the same and that *nothing is secure,* I became more at *rest.*

Resting is not only in the unconscious, dreamlike state of sleeping. As we sleep, we slowly flick the switch that links our thoughts to who we think we are. The mass of scenarios that our thoughts create helps to fulfil the dramas in the movie set of our dreams. Our dreams can be disturbing and sometimes uplifting. If you are flying in a dream, it apparently means you are contented and happy. You are able to escape any hurt or wrongs done to you. When I am anchored in my consciousness, I am at rest and flying. I am comforted knowing that no matter what happens around me when things change in my life, there will always be my consciousness, my *sweet blissful rest.*

The relaxation and rest that comes from external sources is to be appreciated for the pleasure it brings us. When they are our only source of relaxation, though, there can be an underlying reliance to fill the void in their absence. I felt this void or emptiness after returning from holidays. It was a mixture of sadness and the dread of resuming my normal routine. I would look to some future event to offset and suppress these emotions.

It is understandable that we suppress our fears, but this can sap and drain our energy. I experienced this when I had a very anxious period of over two years in which I felt drained most of the time. My physical health was adversely affected and I became tired easily. I could not do the usual things I liked to do. It became noticeable when one weekend I took my grandson on a camping trip. He was an active young boy and needed to be watched all the time, but during the day, I started to fall asleep. Thankfully, he did not run off somewhere in the national park where we had set up camp. I did not concern myself too much with what transpired, and it was only later I realised that my draining energy was the culmination of built-up stress and fear.

In this period I began to experience worrying physical symptoms. I saw a doctor, and after various tests and exploratory surgery they suspected a particular bacterium was causing the problem. I was prescribed heavy drugs to kill the bacterium which caused only further problems. When all this did not work, I turned to natural medicine for a cure. I went on an insecure hunt for anything I could find on the Internet. Both traditional and natural practitioners were left wondering why I was not healing.

True healing comes from the inside. Medication is only a superficial solution, whether it is pharmaceutical or natural. To truly heal, I realised I needed to focus on self-healing, and I worked on the belief that my condition was mainly psychosomatic. I put more trust into my spiritual practice, and this was a beginning of the transforming experience of self-healing.

It was strange though when I put this realisation into practice. I stopped taking all the medication and seeing doctors, and not long after this, my anxiety became extreme again. I did not have any appointments to attend, and I did not have to remind myself to take medication at certain times of the day. I was left with nothing else to rely on but my own abilities. This gave me yet another opportunity to face my fears. As I did this I became more self-reliant and my physical symptoms lessened. My energies increased and I began to feel better. The experience added to the feeling of confidence I was gaining in all my choices. My self-appreciation grew and I felt more at rest.

Opening yourself up to all phenomena can provide you with a newfound excitement into what can be achieved at any level. This opening up contributes to the enjoyment of a new and refreshing perspective in which endless possibilities abound. This period of self-healing presented me with an example of this, and I can light heartedly think of another. I was watching a documentary on the human body that presented a segment relating to the bacterium I had been trying to rid from my body. The segment was about how experiments were showing that a particular strain of this bacterium may offset the effects of asthma. Asthma has had a major effect on many of my family members but fortunately I have not suffered in the grip of this disease. Even though the experiments were not conclusive, I felt wonder in the possibility that having this bacterium may be a blessing and not the contemporary clinical belief that it is harmful.

Possibilities expand with openness. While I was in my cambio in Uruguay, I used to ride my pushbike along the country roadways that surrounded the Isha centre. I was fascinated by all the different types of architecture. There was one particularly charming place that had a sign across the front window which added to its charm. The sign read *Todo Es Posible*, which translates in English to "Everything Is Possible." Whenever I rode past this quaint little dwelling, I would smile in gratitude for being in the moment that captures every possibility.

Gratitude and appreciation can occur on a very simple level. Waking up refreshed every morning after a sound sleep was something I truly appreciated. I was happy to simply *give thanks to a new day*, a day in which everything was possible. I became excited about everything and I wanted to share that enthusiasm.

My enthusiasm was not reciprocated by others though, but I felt compelled to show people how good I felt. As I sensed people's annoyance in my newfound energy I realised this was just another place where I could grow. There is always somewhere that our ego dwells, and in retrospect, what I was doing was just trying to boost my self-image again. I was trying to save the world and make others believe that my way was the right way. Of course, this was just another way of proving my worth. Thankfully, I was able to see it, and I quickly let go of this egoic need. In doing this, I took a further step into the appreciation of my experiences.

Believing a certain way is the right way could be the catalyst for how belief structures and religions are born. Someone chooses to follow a certain path and eventually finds peace in his or her committed practice. That person then wants the world to know and believes that the structure or doctrine will bring peace and save the world. The structure is only the tool; the self is the tradesperson that does the work. There are many tools that will get the same job done.

As I let go of the need to save others, another part of me became free from the boundaries of the mind. With more freedom, I opened up to the possibilities of fulfilling my dreams and desires. My freedom led me *to a place of dreams*. I could not only dream but also walk into that space and make my dreams a reality.

We all have dreams and desires, and it is how we fulfil these that shape our reality. The dreams we have when we are sleeping can be pleasurable or disturbing or even frightening. They are an example of life or our reality with all its weird and wonderful experiences. To shape a reality we truly want, we can give thanks to every part of that reality as it happens in each moment. With an underlying acceptance of life's impermanence we can fulfil our dreams and wake each day to *give thanks again and again and again.*

Chapter 7

Fire

A light, a brightness, a passion,
A fire that will not destroy,
Smouldering away inside,
Waiting to join and ignite.

Embers smothered by patterns,
Sometimes smoke is all you see.
Where there is smoke, there is fire.
Burn, fire, burn.

Sparked by presence,
Fuelled with intention,
A potential radiating greatness,
Let the fires become one.

One of the things that became noticeable at the end of my cambio was that everyone in the group responded and bounced off each other's energy. It was contagious and reminded me of what St. Paul said in Ephesians 5:14

(HCSB), "Everything exposed by the light is made clear". The light of our consciousness began to shine brightly and clearly. The same feeling or phenomena happened when we were with our spiritual teacher. She radiated consciousness, and we all seemed to feed off that energy.

Her name is Isha Judd, and she was born in my home country of Australia. Like most people, she suffered a great deal before entering a spiritual path. With an abundance of commitment, focus, and passion, she developed a high level of consciousness and started teaching a unique and challenging practice. I call her system the accelerator because, with commitment, you can expand consciousness quickly.

She is not what you expect from an enlightened master, but she teaches spiritual truths. The main one being that love is all there ever is. To see that, you need to anchor into the most compassionate, wisest, most understanding and caring, and most loving part of you, and that is your heart. To achieve that, one needs to be transparent and open and be real with oneself with a strong intention to heal. It means taking full responsibility, feeling and expressing all your emotions, and of course, being committed to change. All the people that took part in the six month program were focused and passionate about raising their consciousness to reach their fullest potentials. It was so gratifying to spend so much time with these committed people. We had the goal of supporting one another in bringing our awareness to a higher level. In doing this, we all were becoming the light, and Isha's glow was showing us the way.

There were times though when this did not seem the case. Everyone in the group had his or her own unique process and experience, and I needed to accept that. Some of those in the group showed me that I had become a spiritual know-it-all. I had to let go of my ideas on how a spiritually conscious person should be. I had developed a combination of arrogance and naivety. This created a lot of tension, and at the time, I felt like falling into a big hole, but this became just another place where I could change and grow.

When you live in close quarters for six months with such a large group, opportunities are always there for growth. I wanted to grow, so I took the opportunities to let go of the parts of me that didn't serve, especially my image and ego. I had read and absorbed so much about consciousness and wisdom, and I was using the knowledge as another way of puffing up my ego. Just to let go of the know-it-all and be myself was a meaningful and freeing insight.

Our image can seem to be an important part of us that we need to keep polished. If we are true to ourselves, we can see that this culturally formed image is largely based on the expectations of others. I was surprised to see that my master and all her wonderful teachers had retained their own unique personalities and ways. My perception and expectation of how a consciously enlightened person should act changed and I was inspired to see these dedicated people just being themselves in the compassionate state of giving. They had let go of their images in the pursuit of their passion to help ignite the fire that was smouldering away inside us.

Our desire to want more and be "more" is strong, and a progressive-driven human spirit burns in us all. We have progressed enormously in this modern world, and there is an ever-increasing number of us who want more than what money can buy. Even in our personal relationships, we want more. The only part missing in our searching spirits is the need to go inwards and go deeper and just be with ourselves. To do this can be daunting and is not on most people's agendas—that is, until there is nowhere else to look. Going inwards was confronting and challenging, but it has given me the greatest gift of all. It has shown me that underneath the ego and intellect's dominance, there is my fire.

In our bid to be "more", our fires can seem as if they will destroy us at times. Gaining comfort in the fact that they are *fires that will not destroy* can help us push beyond the boundaries and rules set by the mind. The mind will try to extinguish our fires, but our hearts will show us how to *join and ignite* in a universal desire of unity.

The conditioned patterns that we have developed in our lives can smother our fires, and *sometimes smoke is all we see* in the confusion of trying to be ourselves and conform. This can leave only the *embers* of our fire glowing occasionally. Following your heart will clear the smoke, so your fire will be exposed. All that is needed is the intention to keep the fire going by fuelling it with your consciously driven passion.

Intention can have such an impact on our present state of awareness. Just to have the intention of achieving something can boost our moods even if we fall short

I hear conversations about the wonder of evolution and nature, I sense my fascination is experienced by others as well. This fascination can be expressed on a personal level if we appreciate our own potential to evolve to a more loving species.

All the parts of the natural world flow in a state of being and not in a state of reasoning. *Trees don't question what is happening to them, nor do birds disrupt* the natural flow of life; they just accept. We all have moments when our lives duplicate this and everything just seems to flow effortlessly. Moments like this can expand even more when you can sense your *heart's calling is at its peak* with your strongest desires waiting to be experienced. This experience can manifest by not reasoning or judging but by just flowing.

Whenever I do not flow, I become tense as I try to organise in an overly excessive manner. This can get very draining. My focus then is to *just be* in the moment and enjoy. I do not get caught up in what I *have* to do. My energy then changes as enjoyment becomes the gauge to my presence.

One of the components that helps bring about the acceptance of being in the moment is giving. When at the Isha centre, we all performed some form of service, and it was in service that I started to experience what it meant to *just be* in the moment. Concentrating solely on the task at hand puts you in a natural therapeutic state of presence. The service was voluntary, but as I found out, giving in this way stopped me from worrying about what I had to do next. I was giving in the service of something

I was passionate about, and this gave me the pleasant experience of just flowing.

There will be times when our pasts have a deep effect on us, and it is difficult to stop ourselves from projecting into the future, but if we can see where this might cause us to suffer, we can make the choice to enjoy and *just be*. Situations do expose deep emotions, but I have found that I can embrace these emotions by bringing a deeper form of appreciation into the present. The effect of the past then passes quickly.

In clearing my emotional baggage of my past I was able to move through the hurts and gain a clearer understanding of myself. There are many ways to do this, and some even say it is not necessary to delve into our pasts in order to gain emotional stability. If the intention is to be more present in whatever approach we choose, then the outcome will have a more sustainable quality to it. To have the intention is enough initially; the state of presence will grow from there.

To be in a state of presence constantly is experienced by a few rare individuals. It is an experience I adhere to, and my focus towards being as present as I can has turned into an uplifting experience. As my intention to be present gets stronger, the choice to let go of the thoughts of past and future becomes easier. Anything else but being present is unproductive, and it can keep you caught in the turmoil of blaming and negativity without a clear direction.

There are some parts of our lives that require our fullest attention where our *reasoning minds* are needed.

No Stone Unturned

It is when our minds overshadow those parts that we lose the spontaneity and vibrancy of life. It can be difficult to let go of the urge to do things in a certain way, but the joy of life can get lost in the doing. I was frequently lost in whatever I was doing. My doubts and lack of confidence would undermine my abilities. I was often nervous about making mistakes, and my need for approval contaminated my achievements. This was my mind playing out its protective role of my past, and whatever I was trying to do became a frustrating chore.

When we become frustrated, it might seem as if things are in disarray. This is a time we can look to how the natural world just flows. Flowers are *arranged in disarray* in their natural state, but they have a presence and *a beauty that requires nil*. Our natural state, on the other hand, can get lost in all the things we need to *do*. I believe that when we look at the beauty of a flower, we are looking into our own beauty and our own presence. It is easy to see a flower's beauty but difficult to see our own. The beauty gets masked by the requirements of conforming to our outside environment.

When my need to *do* becomes excessive and I get caught up in trying to prove my worth, I put my attention to the internal space of my heart. Our lifestyles have become more and more fast paced, and it is this internal space that will give us a place to rest. With mental ill health on the rise and relationships becoming increasingly strained, the *heart's calling is at its peak* in the personal and universal need for peace.

It is obvious that history just keeps repeating itself with all the senseless violence that gets played out in the name of a nation's need to protect. We only need to switch on our televisions to see how this is portrayed around the world. Sadly, this violence and emotional turmoil does not happen only among nations but on a domestic and individual level as well. Individual inner transformation and personal responsibility is where the source of the violence can be eliminated.

To have a harmonious world does not mean that there will be no more suffering. We can begin to create it with a passionate intention to heal and accept life as a celebration of growth. To rely on others, especially our leaders and politicians, to take responsibility and show us a way to a better world is not realising our own value. Our leaders' egoic requirements to conform to an image that they have unconsciously created are much greater than ours as they struggle to enforce their agendas. To keep an image in place takes up a lot of energy, and life without an image will cause our *terrified minds* to object to the unknown. We are all the same, even our leaders, and if we are *guided by seeing that love from within*, we can then spread that love by a consciously driven passion of unity.

Life can get so confusing, and like politicians, we battle with what is best for all. The meaning and purpose of our existence can be tested on a regular basis. If we try to shape our existence in a controlled manner and do not realise the perfection of it, we can miss the enjoyment of life. Flowers have no need to be a certain way, and look at how perfect they are. They just grow and keep evolving, and their evolution is something to be marvelled at. The way we have evolved is amazing as well, and we can take the path to follow our hearts and *just be* in the perfection of every moment.

To see perfection in ourselves is difficult. We are heavily influenced by culture to believe that we are far from perfect. Our patterns develop around what we have experienced, and our intellects create who we are as these patterns slowly get cemented firmly in place. I had to trust in what I was aiming for as I began to do the work to shift my patterns. In *trusting like never before* my *terrified mind* objected to the unknown. It was all new to me and meant being fully aware of the patterns that had previously sustained me. Thankfully, I did trust, and it was in trust that I could envelope my old patterns with more loving and gentle new ones.

Changing to a life in which we can *just be* is a slow process, but with trust as one of the main focuses, this change will happen. There will be times when thing are difficult and may not seem perfect, but we can *just be* ourselves in all our *disarray*, in all our dramas, in all our pain and anguish, and in all the good parts that people tell us we have but we do not see. The perfection then lies in the *being* and not so much the *doing*. The desires and urges that we have to live a full life can shape the change we want in the world. We can learn not only from world history but also from our own past history and experiences and make conscious choices with these as our guide.

The word *be* is such a simple yet beautiful word. We can *be* anything we want to *be*. We can *just be* ourselves in our perfection. We can grow to *be* "more" loving and compassionate by being more receptive and open and showing our real selves. We can live our truth by being real with others. We can *be* more responsible with less blame. We can *be* happy and just choose to *be* in the moment with all its ups and downs. We can simply *just be*.

Chapter 9
Choice

Choose for freedom, and choose to live.
Open up your heart so you can give.
Soar the valleys and find clean air.
Climb the mountain; I'll see you there.

Realising our hearts' desires is the essence of a fulfilling life. The desire might be to be successful, to find peace and happiness, to raise a family, or the many other natural urges that motivate us. To love and be loved are among the strongest motivating longings of all. They are an instinctive primordial and unconscious choice that can move the earth. In making a conscious choice we are choosing *for freedom* that comes from the heart.

In many of my choices, I always had a strong desire to be different. The influence that society had on my intellect was a major barrier to fulfilling my heart's desire. It seems like a paradox, but my heart was always patiently waiting for me to make the choices to follow its direction.

As I developed the ability to watch my thoughts, I realised that some of my choices were not in my best interest. If it seems as if I have made a mistake, I let go of these thoughts, as they will only trigger suffering. I replace them with ones that generate peace in an exciting opportunity for growth. Treating them as experiences and not mistakes has taught me that I can grow from these seemingly wrong choices.

My heart and consciousness are my teachers, and they hold the key to the fulfilment of what I truly want. They give me the clarity to see when my mind or the little voice in my head produces thoughts that hold me back. When there is an emotion around a choice to be made and doubts and fears come, I know it is time to go inwards and look for the answer. If my mind adds a thought to the emotion, this causes me to suffer. My thoughts can then evoke many restrictions and boundaries, and with this comes loss of freedom. When I watch my thoughts, I *can choose for freedom and choose to live.*

When my energy levels are low it is usually my mind's voice trying to be the governing force. When I choose intuitively from my heart, with its lighter voice, my energy is different. Of course I use my mind to oversee all the practical and creative parts of my life but when the little voice of my mind sabotages any choices that would be in my best interest, my plans get adversely affected. When this happened I would often go back to a comfortable place as my anxieties increased and my achievements would get undervalued. In some cases I even abandoned my plans and settled for mediocrity.

Making conscious decisions that are in my best interest are important. It may seem selfish, but in essence, it is not. Many of my decisions now come from my heart, and this is where love and compassion grow. If I make decisions that are not in my best interest and are instead based on approval and what others think, I am putting myself in a place of compromise. Compromise is the breeding ground for resentment, and it is with resentment that relationships suffer. The relationship will then have the addition of certain unconscious conditions, with either party making choices not for themselves but to suit the other. With conditions we can close each other off in a state that is full of resentment. It is far healthier to love unconditionally and *open up your heart so you can give* in a caring and sharing committed bond.

In my cambio I had an experience of being uncompromising in giving unconditionally to myself. After being in the centre for over four months, I received the news that my mother had died. I did not compromise in my decision to not go back home to attend her funeral. Our mothers have such a unique nurturing connection to us, and when that connection is missing on an earthly level, the grief suffered at such a loss is profound. Even though my emotions were heightened by being engaged in the intense six-month process, I instinctively knew I was in exactly the right place to feel this loss in an uninhibited emotional release.

Choosing to live a healthy and happy life might seem like such a simple thing to do. When my life became so stressful, I lost the enjoyment of living. I was making unconscious choices that kept me confined to my image. Basically, I was not free to just be me. In exploring the places in myself that I had neglected, I realised just how sad they made me feel and why I would have suppressed them. They were the lows or valleys of my life, and they were all part of the journey. In the acceptance of these lows, I became clearer and found the *clean air* of my awareness that set me free of the barriers of the mind. With clarity I was able to make the choices to expose the person I wanted to be. With *clean air* comes the energy needed to climb *the mountain* of life and go for what you want. This is freedom, the freedom to choose.

Climbing the mountain of our dreams and a fulfilled life is filled with many insights and viewpoints that need to be appreciated. At each viewpoint, the infinite landscape of all our possibilities opens up. When we are in the valleys, we get suffocated by our thoughts and emotions. It is in the valleys that we learn how to climb upward to the *clean air* that brings freedom. The valleys or suffering clearly show us the life we do not want. If we *soar the valleys* of our experience and shift the excess weight of negativity, we can ride on all the uplifting currents that our hearts generate. With each rise in the elevation, our consciousness provides the clarity to make the choice to *climb the mountain; I'll see you there.*

Chapter 10
Share

Share the love, and share the pain,
And fear will fall like April rain.
Feel and feel some more;
Freedom is there if you open the door.
Let go and not resist;
It will come if you persist.
Tears may come, and tears may go;
Love is there if you let them flow.
Seize the moment, and truly feel.
Believe in yourself to make life real.
If living in hope is all you perceive,
Then that is all you will receive.
So take control, and make a true choice.
Listen to your heart with its sweet voice.

There is always love to share, and there is always pain to share. The pain of feeling an unpleasant emotion like sadness can be difficult to share, and we can keep the sadness hidden. There is beauty in sadness. The problem in seeing this beauty occurs when a thought gets added to the sadness. Watching your thoughts when feeling sadness makes it easier to *share the pain* and suffer less. In sharing my love and pain, I was pleasantly surprised by people's reactions. Beauty lies in the experiences you have when you open up to the simplicity of feeling and sharing.

Sharing can come from many different situations. When my mother died, there was still something I could share with her, even though I had not seen her for four months. As I cried after hearing of her death, each tear was in honour of her and our relationship. With each tear I let go of the frustration I had with her and her anxious ways. In allowing the tears to come and feeling the loss, I was sharing something special with her. I was sharing our love and pain. It was the beauty in this that helped me overcome the fear and grief with such a loss.

Fear can be a barrier to the enjoyment of loving relationships and the fulfilment of many of our desires. The fear of losing a close family member can unconsciously block the deep connection you want with the ones you love. An open heart will show you that *tears may come and tears may go*, but *love is there if you let them flow.*

In the past I projected my fears onto my family, especially my son and daughter. These fears were generated by many of my concerns, but the main underlying anxious thought was the fear of losing them. Recognising this, I was able to let go of the thoughts and fears and just enjoy their company and the pleasure of a loving relationship.

Relationships will flourish when we remove the fears that propel us into future scenarios of what might happen. Our anxious patterns can leave us with no room to share what we deeply want to express. This expression is such a natural part of us that can be enjoyed in the fulfilment of our hearts' desires. There is a flow to all external natural phenomena, like the wind and rain, and we can be real with ourselves by going with that flow. To be *real* means to share, even our fears. It does take courage to fully share, but we can gain comfort in knowing that if we *share the love and share the pain, fear will fall like April rain.*

Freedom from fear opens up endless possibilities to experience life to the fullest. All I needed to do was to *open the door* to the dark room of my unconscious self and let in the light of my conscious true nature. In opening the rigid door of my past, I began to *feel and feel some more*, and life did become full, without the need for external pleasures. In the past I would try to fill my life with something new or adventurous. This kept me very busy. I would see something that excited me and would be on a focused mission to extend myself in the quest for more excitement.

It is wonderful to extend yourself and experience the excitement of something new. Whenever I extended myself, though, I always felt there was something missing. There seemed to be emptiness in whatever I did, and I tried to fill the emptiness with more adventures. Even after being engaged in an extreme and dangerous sport, which I thought was the ultimate thrill, I fell into that empty space again. Each new adventure was the same, and I would feel unfulfilled and get bored easily.

Facing my fears was an essential part of looking into the emptiness. Walking towards my underlying fears and feeling the emotions that came was my next big adventure. I did not need to pack any luggage to go anywhere to experience this. The opposite was the case; I just needed to go inwards and just be here and now with whatever I was experiencing. In opening the door of my fears, I progressively cleared the baggage of emotions that clouded my perception.

I am fascinated by this clearing process. It is given many names in both psychology and spirituality, but I like to use the analogy of cleaning the window of your mind. I try not to concern myself too much with how it works, but I am humbled in my appreciation of the people that have brought it into my life. They have given me an open ticket to explore this exciting adventure of the mind.

Trust and belief in yourself is needed if you are to face any big adventure. Internal cleansing is the greatest adventure of all. It requires commitment, persistence and the will to look deeply into your fears. I knew I needed to trust to gain the peace I longed for. In facing my fears, I found that *it will come if you persist*. The clearer I became, the more inspiration I had to *seize the moment and truly feel* in any given situation. Each moment can be a mixture of ups and downs. The adventure is to seize each moment as an opportunity to grow and be "more".

Like April rain and everything else the seasons of nature bring me, like warmth and cold, so too are my internal seasons. The contractions and expansions of the external seasons are part of the cycles of life, and my internal cycles are no different. I contract and expand depending on certain conditions. Resisting my internal cycles and what they bring is like trying to manipulate the weather. To change I needed to experience everything.

The opportunity to experience everything is always there. Every situation creates the different cycles of our beings, and it just depends on what resistance we have to them and the choices we make that determine how we flow with them. There are times when we are in the middle of the storm, and there are times when we bask in the warmth of a sunny day. I was in the middle of a storm when I was trying to make the decision whether to commit to my cambio. I had many doubts and fears, and it felt as if I were holding back a tidal wave. The wave was my heart calling, and my mind was opposing its force. When I faced the fear and did not resist it, the choice became easier. I then went about planning to be away from home for six months.

There is so much we can all share, and emotions are the purest form of sharing, especially when they are shared from your heart. Showing my emotions has been the best connection to others that anything external can bring. I can share my stories and memories, but they have fleeting value. When I share my emotions by simply expressing and feeling them, I am sharing the best gift of all: myself. In sharing all that I have, I am giving to others, and in doing so they can see the real me. If they share their emotions, I can see their real essence as well.

Underneath the superficial masks of our images we are all the same. We are humans just sharing human experiences.

There is a need to *believe in yourself to make life real*. Self-belief brings with it a full life. Being real, being open, being vulnerable, and speaking the truth are all attributes that enhance self-belief. With these attributes the defence fields of our images will fall away naturally. We will attract rather than experience the hurt of repulsion.

We all have moments when life just feels wonderful for no apparent reason. Living from my heart has given me a conscious insight into being in the moment. By not resisting any emotions and instead accepting their presence, we can extend that moment more and more. Each moment can be seized by flowing with everything in a celebration of life.

When you only hope for pleasurable experiences, then *living in hope is all you will receive*. Hope is the future, but what is happening right now is the way to salvation. The hope of feeling something better when there is a disturbing emotion to be felt will push the present moment away. All that is needed is to *take control and make a true choice* in the acceptance and non-judgement of the emotional roller-coaster ride of all our experiences. A space is then created for what the heart may bring. The solution to the peace we want will subtly be answered when we open up this space and *listen to the heart with its sweet voice*.

Chapter 11

The Afternoon

There comes a time in one's life
To walk away from the worry and the strife.
Will it be as we thought?
Could it turn all to nought?

Bring on the change; bring on the new.
It can seem strange with a different view.
There might be grey, there might be old,
But there is always wisdom to be told.

To sacrifice and suffer is part of the game,
For the truth is we are all the same.
We have basked in the glory of the morning's light,
And it is the afternoon that gives us such delight.

Thoughts affect our moods and can give us a high or a low and all the other feelings and emotions in between. Our thoughts have a heavy influence on the choices and actions we make. We become our thoughts as they shape an identity that comes with a name and a birthplace. They can give a false impression of who we think we are. Hidden somewhere beneath the identity is a childlike version that is spontaneous and has the natural carefree trait of simply being in the moment.

This identity or image is a like an intact fragile edifice that is exposed to external forces out of its control. *There comes a time in one's life* to take a step back and see how keeping this image requires so much time and energy. The external forces or surrounding environment of our lives contribute to the amount of time we give this pursuit. When these forces are matched by the abundance of our internal forces, their effects are lessened considerably. This abundance is affected by how much focus we put on the thoughts that do not serve us. These thoughts can add a fabricated anxious state to the primordial sensation of fear if we project too much into the future with unrealistic scenarios. We can simply ask ourselves, *Will it be as we thought?* as we let these thoughts pass like clouds through our minds. Without these thoughts and predictions there are fewer unforeseen obstacles to the joy of life.

My thoughts became excessive to the point where I truly believed them. Thankfully, I chose to *walk away from the worry and the strife* and let the unproductive thoughts drift harmlessly by. The fear-driven predictions and scenarios that I created in my head were sometimes very dramatic, and I would play out a frightened role in the movie set of my mind. As a more alert and creative scriptwriter of this movie, I can use the power of words in a refreshed and renewed dialogue of my own creation. The movie set then takes on a whole new look.

The childlike true nature that we have grown separate from has been deeply affected by how we are supposed to act and behave. This pattern that has been instilled in us creates our perception of life. We look at life through the clouded distortion of conforming to our culture. If we can see this and change, what we perceive changes as well. Even though *it can seem strange with a different view,* it is worth the challenging ascent through the dark forest of our emotions to view life in a new way, especially when the old view causes needless suffering.

When I started to change my perception, it did seem strange, even to the extent that I thought I was going crazy. Of course, this was just the mind creating more thoughts to keep me believing in the false "me." The answer was to not believe the thoughts and instead trust in my choices. The knowledge I had absorbed on my spiritual path provided me with a firm, supportive backup. It was a combination of this accumulated knowledge and trust that accelerated my changing perception. As I changed, I became confident enough to *bring on the change* and *bring on the new,* the newness of a purer perspective.

We are so affected by our pasts that what we want to achieve can get sabotaged and become an unclear, grey area of confusion. To let go of my soul-destroying thoughts and the effects of my past, I realised that *there may be grey* and *there may be old* before I gained a clearer understanding of how to consciously fulfil my goals.

My old patterns were the barriers that held me back, and I often left projects unfinished. I had an abundance of support in breaking down these barriers, and I am grateful for the compassion and wisdom that was bestowed on me. We only have to open up to all the wonderful support that is out there to realise *there is always wisdom to be told*. There is always a lighter and brighter way to view the gloom of doubt.

My gratitude has grown in many ways, and one of those ways was being grateful for the unrecognised wisdom that was within me. Everyone can trust in the fact that this wisdom is within us all, *for the truth is we are all the same*. We all have suffered, and we all have learned from the suffering and the sacrifices we've made. The experience of this suffering can give us the wisdom to see life *with a different view*. This experience is to be greatly appreciated as it gives us the emotional maturity to be whoever we want to be.

To sacrifice and suffer are part of the game in the playing field of life. It is in this game that we set the rules of our own unique experience. Rules are created mainly by the mind, and if the rules do not serve us, we can simply drop them. The man-made rule of *sacrifice* serves no one and is an unnecessary form of suffering we can choose to discard. The rules I play with now are focused on enjoyment and living the fullest life I can. There is no need for me to sacrifice anything but just simply choose the rules that bring freedom.

As you *bring on the change* and *bring on the new*, your perspective becomes refreshingly sharper, and you see yourself differently. Each fresh morning becomes enlivened with each potential opportunity we can create. We can be re-energised with the new day knowing *we have basked in the glory of the morning's light* of our experiences. It is these experiences that bring with them the deep wisdom to feel at ease with whatever happens in each and every moment. The *morning's light* can shine through our fears whenever the mind tries to create the darkness of doubt.

To be completely human and fully alive is to have the acceptance of all the emotions that are there to be felt. With this acceptance comes the delight of knowing we can cope with life's unexpected events. We can even go beyond coping or just survival into a time of thriving. Each situation is like a refreshing morning that brings a new outlook in which we can learn and gain more wisdom. With this wisdom, we will thrive as we drift into the afternoon of our lives, for it is *the afternoon that gives us such delight,* the delight of knowing we are growing more and more.

Chapter 12

Life Is a Game

A new game begins when the morning sets in.
If you make all the rules, the afternoon can lie.
No need to take score, no need for a prize.
Find someone to love, and give them what you've won.

In the game of life, there can be *a new game* in every moment. When you wake each morning, it can be a brand-new experience that is not tarnished by all the rules that are set by the mind. All these structured rules hold us back and create the barriers in realising our authentic selves. These mind-created rules even tell us what emotions we need to experience. With too many rules, what you experience with each new game and each new moment is not quite the truth. Each moment becomes false, and the aftermath of each moment is like a *lie* that keeps the set of fear-driven choices and actions cemented in place.

Rules are shaped by our thoughts and create our identities and who we think we should be. In being watchers of our thoughts, we can slowly let go of our identities in the realisation that there is *no need for a prize* or a well-polished image. Without a prize to win there is no need to prove ourselves, and therefore, there is *no need to take score* of right or wrong. There is *no need to take score* of who is better and who is worse in a society that sets accumulated wealth as the gauge to the contentment of life.

Our whole day can flow as we drift into each moment where the morning and afternoon hold no surprises and no expectations. We can let go of the judgements we make with our emotions as we drop the need to take the score of pleasant experiences against the unpleasant ones. In that way, there is no need for what we are experiencing right now to be any other way.

A new game is the fresh, clear morning of a new perspective, in which you feel renewed and uncontaminated by the rules of a conforming society. The rules and their accompanying thoughts are the genesis of suffering. When you acknowledge this, you will see *if you make all the rules, the afternoon can lie*, the lie of self-destructive thoughts. The afternoon is the experience of life we have in a fabricated impression of who we think we should be. With clearer vision the afternoon will transform into the truth of who we really are.

We all have what we need nestled in the depths of our beings. If we look deeply enough underneath our thoughts, we will find what we have always been looking for. That something is love. Love is the greatest prize of all in the game of life, and when we have it, it is ours to give. In extending that love to everyone you *can give them what you've won* in an unconditional gesture of service.

Afterword

In the wonder of evolution we have advanced to the most intelligent of all species. Our progress has been greatly enhanced by use of the abundant external resources that surround us and there are always new and amazing ways that we adapt these resources to fulfil our wants, needs and desires. The human mind seems to have an unlimited potential in what it can achieve but is there a resource that gets largely overlooked in our evolutionary progression? With the untapped internal resource of emotions as a guiding force we have the ability to create a quantum leap in our evolution by exploring the underdeveloped frontier of the mind.

All our stories are filled with emotions in our own unique celebration of life. It is with a deep appreciation and understanding of this resource that can provide us with the natural inheritance of love, the purest form of all emotions.

In a world that at times is challenging and confusing, we can always gain comfort in knowing we have exactly what we need in any given moment. This need will be fulfilled by going inward and taking the leap to follow your heart. The heart has the answers that will bring the joy of life and guide you on *The Path to Freedom*.

For more information on Stephen and his activities and projects visit,

- www.stephenconnor.org
- www.steveconnorandlife.wordpress.com

For the Isha System and RC visit links below

- Isha System Australia on Facebook: www.facebook.com/IshaSystemAustralia
- The Isha System and the Isha Foundation for Peace: www.ishajudd.com
- www.rc.org

It takes courage to get to a place with no boundaries.

About the Author

Stephen is a facilitator for the Isha System, has a diploma in health counselling and is a personal and group fitness trainer. He lives in his home city of Sydney, Australia, and has two children and two grandchildren. He has written plays, including Emo Class, which he aspires to make into a production to tour schools with the hope that it will teach children about the gift of emotions.

CPSIA information can be obtained at www.ICGtesting.com
Printed in the USA
LVOW07s2247120115

422492LV00001BA/33/P